D0397980

Self
and
Soul

A Woman's Guide to Enhancing
Self-Esteem through Spirituality

Adele Wilcox

Daybreak® Books
An Imprint of Rodale Books
New York, New York

Copyright © 1997 by Adele Wilcox
Cover photograph copyright © 1997 by Janice L. Sugarman

All rights reserved. No part of this publication may be reproduced or
transmitted in any form or by any means, electronic or
mechanical, including photocopying, recording, or any other
information storage and retrieval system, without the written
permission of the publisher.

Daybreak is a registered trademark of Rodale Press, Inc.

Printed in the United States of America on acid-free ∞,
recycled paper ♻

Cover designer: Jane Colby Knutila
Cover photographer: Janice L. Sugarman
Interior designer: Faith Hague

Library of Congress Cataloging-in-Publication Data

Wilcox, Adele.
    Self and soul : a woman's guide to enhancing self-esteem through
spirituality / by Adele Wilcox.
        p.   cm.
    Includes bibliographical references.
    ISBN 0–87596–446–X hardcover
    1. Women—Religious life. 2. Spiritual life—Christianity.
3. Self-esteem—Religious aspects—Christianity. I. Title
BV4527.W544 1997
248.8'43—dc21   97–724

Distributed in the book trade by St. Martin's Press

2 4 6 8 10 9 7 5 3   hardcover

Contents

Preface

"Why don't you ever preach about hell and judgment?" The day Marilyn came into my study and asked me her question sticks vividly in my mind. Marilyn attended my small-town church in Pennsylvania for almost a year. Shy and retiring, she always sought opportunities to help others. However, her aid was intense, as if she were working off some indebtedness.

My response was a story about another woman named Gerry. Gerry had been active in a church where I had worked years before. As I climbed into the pulpit to give one of my very first sermons, she approached me with a twinkle in her eye. "Give them heaven," she advised. Throughout my years of ministry, I listened to Gerry in my mind as I checked my notes to ensure that they contained a message of good news. This underlying theology of life permeated my ministry.

Somehow in her past, Gerry absorbed this message of joy. She was a secure, self-assured woman who was not afraid to speak publicly about issues of importance to her. Gerry internalized goodness for herself and gave it to others.

Marilyn, in contrast, had digested another philosophy of life—one that told her she was "less than," deserving of condemnation by others and by God. Despite her willingness to be of service, this underlying theme seeped through. Her service stemmed not from joy but from fear.

Over the years, I listened carefully and observed others as they talked about spiritual issues and the subsequent impact of their beliefs on their lives. I noticed a pattern. Self-assured people internalized a loving, kind God into their sense of self. Insecure people, however, talked about a God of judgment, a God outside of themselves who looks harshly upon humanity in general and the individual specifically.

Questions surfaced. In what way does spirituality affect self-esteem? If, in fact, a correlation exists between self-esteem and spirituality, can self-esteem be enhanced by developing a loving, interior spirituality?

Certainly this had been true in my own life. As my theology evolved, I looked at myself in new ways, coming to understand—intellectually and emotionally—that the divine is centered within me. I know that I am holy—not the unholy person that I often felt I was because of my childhood environment and the message of unworthiness I received from my church.

In many ways this did not change the reality of my world. As a woman, I am still often discounted by others. However, I no longer see this discounting as a reflection on me but on the other's lack of understanding of God's presence within me. I still need to work for equal pay and other justice concerns. But my ego is no longer fractured in the process. With the Gerrys of this world, I stand tall in the struggle.

From these questions, observed patterns, and further musings emerged *Self and Soul*. It deals with self-esteem through a spiritual dimension. It invites the reader into spiritual territory to emerge from the journey as a more self-loving, self-confident person. *Self and Soul* is for Marilyn and all who feel "less than."

Dushore, Pennsylvania
November 1995

Acknowledgments

I've always been fascinated by acknowledgment sections of books—until I wrote my own. I now realize how many people are important to the production of a single listing in the card catalog of a library. For me the important people include my husband, John Kirk, who encouraged me every step of the way; Sarah Casey, Director of Schuylkill Women in Crisis, who believed that the concepts found in this book would help her clients; Peggy Halsey of the Women's Children and Family Ministries of the United Methodist Church who supplied grant money for the initial project; members of my critique group who plowed through each word with me: Carol Hartley Shaw, Margaret Bayer, Patricia Calisher, Maryann Friend, Jean VanDyke, Mary Beth Voda, and Candy Zulkosky; colleague and author Patricia Brown; my excellent and persistent agent, Sheree Bykofsky; and my insightful and skillful editor at Rodale's Daybreak Books, Karen Kelly.

Rugged individualism is an American illusion. I know firsthand that more than my effort was required for *Self and Soul* to become a reality. Thanks to all of you.

1

As the Village Goes

*"Sometimes it takes years to really
grasp what has happened to your life."*
—Wilma Rudolph[1]

Prevailing Wisdom or Inner Wisdom

The mother cradled her in her arms and carried her to yet another doctor. "I'm sorry, there's nothing more that we can do for your daughter," the mother heard once again. But the mother refused to believe the prevailing prognosis that her daughter would not recover from polio. Night after night she massaged the paralyzed legs. Night after night she prayed. At the age of nine, Wilma Rudolph's braces were removed from her legs.

Nine years of defying the cultural norm. Nine years of encouragement. Nine years of massages. Nine years of prayer.

Rudolph ran and played. She excelled in basketball. But most of all she excelled in speed. In 1960 Rudolph became the first woman to win three gold medals in track and field at the Summer Olympics.

What would have happened if Rudolph's mother had accepted the doctors' verdicts? What would have happened if Rudolph's mother had listened to prevailing wisdom rather than her own inner wisdom? What would have happened without a faith greater than the norm?

What happens when we accept what others tell us even though an inner voice struggles to be heard? What happens when we mold ourselves to normative standards of behavior set for us? Could we, too, end up wearing braces—emotional braces—our whole lives rather than winning at this race we call life?

So Go the Children

"I grew up believing what everyone else believed. It never occurred to me until I was 30 that options existed." Marguerite twirled her long black hair around her index finger as she talked. "Sure, I had one social studies teacher who loved my research on the inner city and encouraged me and said that I could become anything I wanted. The problem was that what I wanted was to be a beautiful curvaceous blond like Marilyn Monroe so that I could capture some kind of Prince Charming. It was pretty obvious"—she pulled her hair out for everyone to see—"that blond was something that I would never be. So, of course, I thought that it was impossible for me to become anything that I wanted. I wanted the community norm for women. I thought that it would bring me happiness. Ha! What a misconception that was."

Marguerite is not alone. Community, or societal, norms may change, but whatever they are at the time, they shape our lives enormously. In fact, many things that we take as truth are merely the sum total of community belief.

Think of how we view aging. Carl Lewis was considered old for the 1996 Summer Olympics. He was 36 when he won his last gold medal—10 years past what should have been his prime.

Everyone knows that runners are at their peak in their twenties and that it is downhill from there. Everyone knows that the body cannot do at 30 or 40 what it can do at 20. Everyone, that is, but the Tarahumara Indians in Mexico.

Certain members of this tribe run the equivalent of a marathon or more every day. What is fascinating is that this tribe believes that the best runners are in their sixties. Researchers found that the tribe's reality corresponds to its belief system: The best lung capacity, the best cardiovascular fitness, and the highest endurance are in 60-year-old runners.[2] Like so many of us, they never question their basic belief. The old runners keep running.

Marguerite and her friends began naming stereotypes about women that they learned as young girls—beliefs that they never questioned for years. It didn't take long to compile a list. Women have been internalizing them for decades:

- Girls are better in art; boys are better in math.
- Girls prefer dolls to soccer.
- Beauty is a girl's greatest attribute.
- Mechanical jobs, like fixing the car, are best left to men.
- Women are the natural caretakers of children.
- Men are leaders; women are followers.
- When a woman is in a difficult situation, a man will save her.
- Women do not belong in the military.

In her 1996 book, *It Takes a Village*, First Lady Hillary Rodham Clinton contends that raising children encompasses both parental and societal responsibility. Clinton defines the village as the network of values and relationships that support and affect our lives.[3] These can be either positive or negative. Consequently, the village, or society, influences children immeasurably, and our cultural values permeate formative minds. Regardless of whether two middle-class parents raise 2.5 children in suburbia or a poor, single mother struggles to bring up 4 children with financial assistance, parents have only a limited amount of control over what their children absorb from outside. The village's influence will seep in.

Perhaps Clinton's book could have been titled *As the Village Goes, So Goes the Child*. When the village believes that 60-year-olds are the best runners, they are strong runners. When the village believes that beauty is worth dying for, women die (through anorexia, failed plastic surgery, malnutrition). When the village believes that men are number one, women assume a secondary position. When the village believes that women belong at home, women stay home or feel guilty about going to work. When the village believes that financial success provides validation, villagers seek monetary gains to bolster themselves.

Are village, or cultural, norms harmful? Some are obviously helpful. When the village norm says that a red light means "stop," I can be sure that cars in opposite lanes will stop while I drive through my green light.

Some norms, such as those described by Marguerite and her friends are restrictive. Women can excel at math and at changing tires. Telling them that they can't affects how they feel about themselves.

Telling women that they are not competent leaves them feeling unsure. Telling women that only men can save them renders them powerless. Telling women that beauty is their most important asset sets them up to compare and compete with other women over inherited attributes that they cannot control.

Village norms are more than skin-deep. They penetrate a person's soul. They become more than cultural messages. They invade the spirit.

The overriding effect of the village norms of middle America are not subtle. They shape women's senses of self and leave them empty of substance and dependent on others to fill the void. Self-esteem does not have a chance to develop positively without overcoming a myriad of influences.

When women are asked about their spiritual lives, similar issues arise. Women learn about saintly stereotypes in church or synagogue. They can never match the images of the perfect, holy women of the past.

Both self-esteem and spirituality suffer in a cultural network that denigrates women. Marguerite and her friends know that more is possible. They know that life would be more fulfilling if they could fill the empty places in their gut hollowed out by denigrating messages. Indeed, they have had fleeting moments of connectedness. What they want is for those fleeting moments to last. Is it possible to enhance both self-esteem and spirituality? How?

The Connection

Spirituality and self-esteem are integrally related. Both concern internal well-being. Both channel how we respond to the world. A sense of self arises from deep within one's soul—the solar plexus, the gut, the place where we feel deeply. I am amazed that so many writers of self-esteem books ignore the connection. Does a need to be scientific cause these authors to miss a major link? To be sure, many religions have been detrimental to self-esteem, a sad irony of efforts to organize faith systems. Psychologists have earned millions working with people recovering from strident, self-deprecating religious teachings. Our inner selves can free us and enhance our lives. Sadly, some religious practices can destroy that very self.

If spirituality concerns our vital spirit or life force, and the self is the identity or personality of a given person as distinct from others, then it is obvious that the two are interconnected. Who could be more self-assured than Sojourner Truth, a nineteenth-century abolitionist and escaped slave; Mother Teresa of Calcutta; or Peace Pilgrim, American crusader for world peace? For each of these women, self-esteem grew out of a spiritual awakening and manifested itself in an energized, purposeful life. They did not ride away into the confines of a castle but into the center of the living, breathing, conflicted world.

We cannot escape into God to feel better about ourselves. To do so is hiding. Rather, as we unite with the spark of divinity that exists within us, we absorb energy from the union of self and spirit and receive strength to tackle the barriers that suppress our sense of worth.

Low Self-Esteem Has a Face and a History

Jeannette came to the self-esteem group that I led because "I've been told my whole life how awful I am, and I want to stop believing that. My ex used to put me down in front of the kids all of the time, and now they don't respect me. I want to learn how to earn back their respect." Jeannette did not outwardly fit the role that she described. She was a tall, slender woman with a welcoming smile and blond hair pulled back into a braid. As a child, Jeannette attended a traditional, conservative church with her parents. She heard both at church and at home that a woman's main function is to take care of the children and obey her husband. Her mother was obviously unhappy in her role, but Jeannette heard her cope by repeating simple statements such as, "God doesn't give you more than you can handle," or "Sometimes we just don't understand God's will for us."

Jeannette's father was not a violent man. His emotional absence was his abuse. He focused his attention on Jeannette's two brothers and paid little attention to Jeannette in her childhood years, except to correct her behavior with insulting comments.

Jeannette married Steve as soon as she graduated from high school to escape the emotionally stagnant atmosphere of her home. Steve learned quickly that Jeannette could be controlled by put-downs and rejections. No matter how much she dieted, he called her fat. (Jeannette is a large-boned but well-proportioned woman.) No matter how much she cleaned, he found dirt. If she needed to stay a few moments late at the office, he threw a temper tantrum if dinner was not served promptly at six o'clock, at the same time grilling her accusatorily about her whereabouts. Jeannette stayed with Steve because she had no realistic sense of her ability to cope on her own. She believed that she could not survive without Steve or another man. Finally, when the children were teenagers, Steve threw her against the wall and knocked her unconscious. A friend took her to a shelter where she began to rebuild her life.

Throughout her 35 years, Jeannette absorbed many negative concepts about herself from her mother, father, minister, and husband. It was difficult for her to believe that she possessed the ability to succeed on her own. She was rotten to the core, she said. She believed that she was suffering just like Eve because she was a bad person and a lousy mother.

Jeannette exhibited many signs of poor self-esteem.[4]

⟨ She felt inferior to others and feared failure on her own.

⟨ She tried hard to conform to the role of woman as taught to her and felt guilty when she could not measure up to those standards.

⟨ She apologized frequently, even for things that were not her fault.

❬ Jeannette constantly put down other people, attempting to look better in her own eyes.

❬ She could not easily accept genuine compliments from her friends.

❬ Her fear of rejection meant that she tolerated emotional abuse in her marriage for 15 years.

When asked to describe her inner self, Jeannette at first was able to name only a hollow space, a vast emptiness that she felt. Later she added that a wet lump sometimes sat in that space. The lump was heavy and unmoving. It weighed her down and became yet another burden to drag around.

Here are the key questions: Is it possible for Jeannette to fill her hollow space? Can she fill herself not with "wet lumps" that need dragging but with self-approval, self-acceptance, self-confidence, and self-love that give vigor to living rather than deplete energy? Where would such self-validation come from? What would it look like?

Can we, after being taught for our entire lives to find validation outside ourselves—whether from parents, teachers, spouse, or God—begin to look within and value what we find?

The answer is yes. Skills that develop this kind of validation can be learned. Spiritual exercises can be practiced. Self-care can begin. Self-esteem can grow. The following chapters will provide information and suggestions for change that will both deepen your spirituality and strengthen your self-esteem.

The Search Goes On

Bill, the father of a 16-year-old girl, came to me and bemoaned, "My wife and I tried hard to raise our daughter to think for herself and overcome the cultural notions for women. But when she hit her teenage years, she proved the studies true. Her life is centered around boys and what she can do to win them. We only hope that this is a stage and that she will remember our teachings. In junior high her extra energy went to her science project. Now her scientific knowledge goes into the study of makeup solutions so that she can match some ideal of beauty. What's a parent to do?"

Louis Harris and Associates polls reveal that in the 1990s, 90 percent of women want to change something about their appearance.[5] Weight is the most often mentioned feature (87 percent), and 29 percent would like to overhaul their entire appearance.

These polls tend to concentrate on White American women. There are surveys that show young Black women as having higher self-esteem than young White women. In an interview in *On the Issues*, attorney Barbara Arnwine, executive director of the National Lawyers' Committee for Civil Rights under Law, says that unlike White women, "we have a tradition of standing outside of the rest of the culture and defining ourselves." Other polls, according to Arnwine, indicate that "Black women express more personal satisfaction, although African-American women are also the least happy specifically about their wages, their salaries, and their chances for promotion."[6]

Is it possible, almost 30 years after the start of the women's movement, that young (mostly White) girls are still growing up receiving denigrating messages in movies, television, and other media presentations? It is very possible. It is made possible by a culture that is re-focusing on "family values" without explicitly naming those values. Discussions concerning family time do not specify who will spend time in nurturing roles. Implicit in these political conversations are gender roles that have been dubbed tradition, a word that gives validity to an idea. The corporate world is working more hours and putting in longer days. Corporate management is still a strong male majority. We know who is to be home filling the void—Mother—even if she has to work.

Reaching for the Self: Definitions of Self-Esteem

Professionals provide many different definitions of self-esteem.

« William Appleton suggests that self-esteem is the reputation that you have with yourself.[7]

« Paul Hauck, a clinical psychologist and author of *Overcoming the Rating Game* is convinced that what others think of us is not as important as what we think of ourselves.[8]

❦ In *The Six Pillars of Self-Esteem*, psychotherapist Nathaniel Brandon writes, "Self-esteem is the integrated sum of self-confidence and self-respect. It is the disposition to experience oneself as competent to cope with the basic challenges of life and as worthy of happiness."[9]

❦ Psychotherapist Linda Sanford and Mary Donovan, co-authors of *Women and Self-Esteem*, tell us that "the self-concept or self-image is the set of beliefs and images we all have and hold to be true of ourselves. By contrast, our level of self-esteem (or self-respect, self-love, or self-worth) is the measure of how much we like and approve of our self-concept."[10]

Definitions of self-esteem abound. Professionals even spend time discrediting others' definitions to forward their own. What I know is that if you ask women if they understand self-esteem, they may not be able to verbalize a definition, but they know what you mean. And they know if theirs is good or bad.

We know that we would like:

❦ To stand with our heads held high
❦ To feel optimistic about our lives
❦ To feel confident that what we say and think has value
❦ To feel creative and productive in our work and our personal lives
❦ To have harmony and peacefulness within ourselves

We know what high self-esteem looks like. We all desire it for ourselves.

Exercises: Remembering

1. Who did you want to "grow up to be" when you were a little girl? Did that change over the years? Write down these various aspirations and how they impacted your adulthood.

2. Keep track of commercials on television for one week. Write down the messages that they give concerning how you should look, dress, keep house, do laundry, and cook. How have these messages defined or constricted who you are?

3. Make a list of the messages that you received from your family during your childhood and teenage years of what it means to be a woman. For example: Girls don't fight. Looks are more important than intelligence. Men get the biggest piece of meat at dinner.

Were they conflicting? How do they compare with the messages from movies, television, magazines, and literature?

2

The Clash
of Faith and Self

"We piece together what we will believe in."

—Carol Flinders, author of *Enduring Grace*[1]

❦

The Message or the Medium?

One of Satan's workers watched in horror as a man climbed to the top of a mountain, reached up, and seized Truth. The worker scurried off to Satan to report his findings. Satan was unruffled. "Don't worry," he told the underling. "I'll convince him to institutionalize it."[2]

Institutionalized religion, the organization and administration of faith, is problematic for women. It assimilates the culture of its origin and justifies that culture. A patriarchal culture, where men's beliefs and rules are the norm, will produce a patriarchal religion. Faith gleaned from religious upbringing can provide interior strength; while at the same time, traditions imposed by the same institution can stifle growth, destroy a sense of self, and injure one's esteem.

As a little girl, I loved church. I remember being the first in third grade fulfilling the requirement to memorize the Apostles' Creed in order to qualify to sing in the junior choir. I loved the mystery and ritual. When my canary died, I led a group of 10-year-olds in solemn procession around the backyard for a fitting burial in a shoe box. I had such a good time that I dug Peetie up and repeated the ceremony. Something pulled me into the realm of the unknown. I learned to sing Bible school songs enthusiastically. I knew the characters and plots of Bible stories. But as I grew into a teenager and a young adult, I did not realize what else I had unknowingly absorbed.

Subconsciously, I learned that:

❨ I had very little value. A girl was not allowed to be president of my youth fellowship. I got to be vice-president and do the work while a boy held the title and received the recognition.

❨ Even though the offering plates weren't very heavy, women only carried them on Mission Sunday.

❨ I should be good, right, and perfect, and if I had a problem, it was a moral weakness.

(Even though my denomination had been ordaining women for quite a few years, most church people really did not want a woman as their minister. In fact, it was quite a while before I even knew that women could be ordained.

(Despite the preacher's sermons about love, people from other races or economic classes did not seem welcome in our church.

(God was a male and didn't look or feel much at all like I did.

I wonder if I had been a boy, would I have been encouraged to enter ministry as a youth? Besides active involvement in all possible activities, including retreats, choir, summer camp, and youth fellowship, I often volunteered to lead devotions at youth meetings. The format gave me an opportunity to work out my beliefs with others. Instead, I was 35 before a woman minister suggested what should have been obvious but had escaped even me: "You should go to seminary."

Relearning

It was in seminary that I began to unravel what had been oppressive theology for me and for many other women. Scholarship from both female and male professors helped me unlearn old and incorrect teachings.

Here are some things that I now know. Have you learned:

❮ That there are new interpretations for the old "it's the woman's fault" lines from Genesis?

❮ That the Hebrew word translated as "helpmate" to describe Eve's relationship to Adam means a helper within an equal relationship, not the subservient relationship espoused in traditional faiths?

❮ That the passages most often used against women found in Ephesians 5 ("Wives, be subject to your husbands as you are to the Lord") and Colossians 3 ("Wives, be subject to your husbands, as if fitting in the Lord") were probably not written by Paul at all, but were based on Greek codes of Aristotle and were added to the scripture texts later?

❮ That male translators had been selective in early translations?

❮ That the Greek word *diakonos/ia*, which is found eight times in the New Testament, was translated *deacon* when it referred to men, but *servant* when it referred to women?

❮ That women were present at Pentecost?

❮ That women were not only deacons and elders in the early church, but also bishops?

❮ That many of us were taught inaccurate Bible stories by Sunday school teachers? For example, nowhere in the Bible does it indicate that Mary Magdalene was a prostitute. I sadly learned when I left seminary that these findings did not matter. Many of them had been discovered, buried, rediscovered, and reburied for years. The need for theology to conform to culture is more important than truth.

I learned, as you may have, too, that my new knowledge could easily be dismissed and trashed as "the work of the devil," or "feminist," which seem to be interchangeable words.

Gerda Lerner, in *The Creation of Feminist Consciousness*, does an excellent job of revealing the repetitious work of generations of women who struggled for insights that had been uncovered before them, only to be suppressed. Thus, when individual women from the Middle Ages up until the twentieth century reinterpreted the Bible, they did so from scratch, without the benefit of previous works.[3]

The pattern continues to a lesser extent today. In my own experience, none of my findings were particularly new in terms of academic biblical studies. The important point in my case was that they were new to me. I wondered, "Why hadn't I been taught this way?" Later my questions changed to "Now that people know, why aren't the teachings changing? Why do other girls have to grow up excluded, marginalized, and put down by their religions?"

Abuse of a Powerful Message

My story seems minor compared to those of other women.

When women are continuously undervalued, self-esteem can waver. But when women are undervalued by an institution representing God, the effects can be devastating.

As both minister and counselor, I have worked with women whose pastors have told them to return to battering husbands and "pray harder," that it was the woman's fault for provoking the husband to anger.

An overwhelming number of women still believe that their lot in life is to suffer because of Eve's sin.

Women raised in fundamentalist Christian churches share books on "Christian marriage," which instruct them that "a wife's primary responsibility is to give of herself, her time, and her energy to her husband, children, and home. . . . There is no blessing for her to be found except as she humbly attaches herself to him."[4]

Catholic women tell me of their struggle to remain within their faith, knowing that their daughters, as they were, are denied admission into the priesthood.

Original Sin

Only 1 staff member in 10 at one domestic violence shelter remembers being taught a positive relationship with God as a child. The others named a variety of ways that sin and guilt were the most prominent ideas that they absorbed from their childhood religious teachings. The spectrum of childhood religions was all-encompassing—

mainline Protestant, Roman Catholic, Eastern Orthodox, Jewish, conservative Evangelical, Christian fundamentalist.

"I was doomed no matter what. Original sin was a part of me, so I must be no good. That is what I was taught," lamented Joyce, whose father had been Baptist and mother, Assembly of God.

Annette, raised a strict Catholic, chimed in, "I remember the old prayer manual, which instructed us to beat our breasts three times as we declared, 'I am not worthy, I am not worthy, I am not worthy.' In fact, I think that it was the same prayer book that had a ritual for women after they had a baby. They weren't to re-enter the church until they had been cleansed by the priest. I think that they were to kneel at the door of the church until they were sprinkled with holy water. My mother told me that she went through that with all five of us.

"You know," she mused, "I can laugh at that now. But I realize that it is really ingrained. My head knows that it's silly, but my insides still tell me that I am unworthy and unclean."

It was Deborah, with her Reform Jewish origins, who taught the women raised in the Christian faiths something new. "I was not taught the concept of original sin. That's something that you Christians have that we don't. Jewish women certainly have their issues, though. After all, our men used to pray daily giving thanks that they were not born women. The Orthodox still do. Our guilt and shame originate deep within our culture."

One of the biggest stumbling blocks to self-esteem for women (and in this case men, too) is not just the practices of the church but its intrinsic theology. Original sin is the concept that people are born flawed, that something intrinsic in human nature is wicked.

Psychotherapist Nathaniel Brandon, author of *The Six Pillars of Self-Esteem*, names the issue clearly and succinctly: "The idea of Original Sin is anti-self-esteem by its very nature."[5]

Yet, original sin haunts those raised in a traditional Christian environment. John Wesley, founder of the Methodist Church and its many branches, listed original sin as one of the six essential doctrines of faith. In fact, he said that Christianity could not exist without it: "A denial of original sin contradicts the main design of the gospel, which is to humble vain man.... If we give this up, we cannot defend either justification by the merits of Christ, or the renewal of our natures by his Spirit."[6] In other words, unless we feel bad about ourselves, the gospel has no merit.

Original Goodness

In sharp contrast is what the mystics, Eastern religions, native religions, and careful reading of Genesis and the Christian gospels teach us: Pro-self-esteem springs from the concept of original goodness. We are born with original goodness, in the image of the divine, and we carry a piece of the divine within ourselves. Our birth is a blessing, a time of rejoicing. We are not inherently unworthy, just as we are not inherently unimportant, unlovely, or undesirable.

This is not to deny that humans do wrong and even sometimes terrible things. They do. Just scanning the evening newspaper or turning on the television reminds us of that. However, we need to remember that our original nature, our spiritual nature, our innate human condition is divine, not evil.

Lonna is a woman eager to hear this message. Her background includes both Latino and fundamentalist Christian upbringing. By the time she was 30 years old, she had been abandoned by her husband for another woman and left to raise two sons by herself. She was also convinced that her problems were all her fault.

"I went to my pastor for help," she recalls. "He told me that it was my husband's right to demand proper respect for him. He told me that I needed to be a better wife, to submit more to my husband, and then I wouldn't have these problems. I tried, but nothing changed. Finally, he did not come home at all, except to pick up his clothes and belittle me one more time."

Heartbroken and afraid, Lonna went back to her pastor again. She was told that divorce was forbidden, and "that I would be committing even more of a sin if I did not get my act together and get my husband to return home. I was helpless. There was no way he was going to return. He told me that he wanted this other woman, that she knew how a woman was to act.

"I felt ashamed to even be around my family. They supported everything that the pastor said. My mother, my mother—can you believe it?—told me that this is what happens to women because of what Eve did. If it weren't for the children, I think that they would have had nothing to do with me. Finally, they did disown me—when I left the church."

Through a friend, Lonna found a pastor who encouraged her to read the Bible for herself.

"He told me that these things weren't all my fault. He showed me some different ways to look at my life. That helped a lot, but I don't go to church even there. There are too many bad memories. And even though I know in my head now that what I was taught when I was growing up isn't true, those teachings are still inside me. It is hard not to feel that I am a wicked person, responsible for the fact that my children's father left us all."

Lonna paused in her story. She sipped water and gathered her thoughts some more.

"It's still hard for me because when I left the church, I had to leave all of my friends there. None of them will have anything to do with me now, except Anna. She still calls, but only to try to get me back, not because she really wants to help me in my own life.

"So, in addition to losing my husband and his financial support, I lost my family and my church. But I had to leave in order to survive. I was going mad staying there."

Lonna remains confused. She wants to raise her children with a faith system but is afraid that the emotional damage that she experienced will also be inflicted on her sons. She doesn't want them to grow up thinking that they have a right to treat women any way they want. Holidays are hard for Lonna because she misses the worship experiences associated with them. Just hearing Christmas carols on the radio can reduce her to tears.

"I do believe in God," she says. "God's just not like the one I was taught."

Lonna was encouraged to join a women's study group that analyzed biblical passages from a woman's perspective. The group responded to her need for worship and began to share times of reflection and prayer together.

"I'm not ready to go to a regular church again," she says. "But I no longer have to separate my belief in God from my day-to-day life in order to survive. I no longer look at myself as evil. I'm a good person. I really am. And now most of the time I believe that."

Another woman, Barbara, sorts through and chooses what pieces of her faith she still honors. She never goes to church on Mother's Day when "I'll hear all of that syrupy stuff about the perfect mother." On the other hand, "I would never miss Easter and the feeling of joy that it gives me. I don't care what the pastor preaches about on Easter. I know the story. I know it was women who dared to go to the tomb when the men were hiding out. That makes me feel powerful."

Religious teachings have strong implications for self-esteem. These teachings did not necessarily occur in church or synagogue but came through the family or culture. Some parents use God-talk to intimidate or punish: "God doesn't like little girls who act like that." Entire cultures use religion to justify dehumanizing behavior for women. Even though it is not in the Koran, women in tribes throughout Africa and elsewhere are told that the Koran teaches female genital mutilation as God's will. Because many are illiterate, these women do not have the means to see that this teaching doesn't exist in their scriptures. The theology has once again conformed to support cultural tradition.

Sorting through these teachings is a first step to change.

Coming or Going

Countless women know the limitations of their faith systems and yet continue to return. Why? What underlying message are women seeking that they believe can be found there? What makes it worthwhile?

For many, the power of God's love keeps drawing them. Like a wildflower in a thicket, the original message of encompassing love continues to poke its head through the briers, beckoning. People yearn to feel that power.

People come for friendships, to accomplish mission work at a level unachievable individually, to participate in positive communal rituals, and to listen expectantly for a new, clear message. Under the haze of patriarchy, status quo, and tradition, shines a beacon of hope. Many cannot resist its pull and endure many abuses, trying to connect with their spiritual selves.

Organizations often lose their original purpose over time as they strive to perpetuate themselves. We see it in many places. The most blatant one today is the health care system. Hospitals have become money-making entities in addition to—and sometimes more than—places to care for the sick. It is not because doctors and nurses don't care about the ill. They simply cannot avoid being caught in the financial ramifications of their decisions.

Religious institutions are no different. Working for the financial survival of a synagogue or church can overtake the original mission. Justifying the culture can supplant the original message, hiding God's grace in the process.

Religious institutions are comprised of people—people steeped in their culture, their upbringing, their own traditions—some good, some not so good. It is up to each person, therefore, to decide for herself whether to come or go on the Sabbath.

THE CLASH OF FAITH AND SELF

Exercises: Moving toward Change

1. Take a sheet of paper and divide it into two columns. On one side, list the positive messages that your worshiping community gave you as you were growing up. On the other side, list the negative messages. Compare the two lists. What feelings do you have as you review them? If you are still practicing the faith of your childhood, name ways that the negative messages have receded, if they have. If you are not practicing, can you explain why?

2. Write down five things that you would like to do for yourself (go back to school, take a bubble bath for two hours). Draw up a plan or set aside a specific time to do them. Then, make a list of things that you do for others that they could do for themselves. Remember that taking care of oneself should not lead to feelings of guilt. Not taking care of others who can care for themselves should not lead to guilt either.

3. With a few friends, read aloud parts of the sacred texts of your faith that deal with women. Discuss if you hear these passages differently now than you were taught. How do you feel when you hear them?

3

The Cohesion of Faith and Self: An Achievable Ideal

"Everybody must learn this lesson somewhere—that it costs something to be what you are."

—Shirley Abbott[1]

※

Street Walking

The poem "Autobiography in Five Chapters" speaks about the hard work of beginning to live life in new ways. It moves from victim mentality to internal responsibility, from hopelessness to confidence, from low sense of self to high capability.

1. I walk down the street.
There is a deep hole in the sidewalk
I fall in.

I am lost . . . I am hopeless.
It isn't my fault.
It takes forever to find a way out.

2. I walk down the same street.
There is a deep hole in the sidewalk.
I pretend I don't see it.
I fall in again.
I can't believe I'm in the same place.
But it isn't my fault.
It still takes a long time to get out.

3. I walk down the same street.
There is a deep hole in the sidewalk
I see it is there.
I still fall in . . . it's a habit
My eyes are open
I know where I am
It is my fault.
I get out immediately.

4. I walk down the same street.
There is a deep hole in the sidewalk
I walk around it.

5. I walk down another street.[2]

SELF AND SOUL

This poem is one of transition, from allowing events to happen to making intentional life choices. Transition occurs when eyes open, when the individual no longer is blind to what is happening to her. Transition occurs when there is acknowledgment that life is not all happily ever after but, instead, full of difficult choices. Transition occurs when there is recognition that one needs to take responsibility, even if it means change—change of the street that one walks down, change in whom one walks with, change in how one looks at the street.

This change begins as an internal process. It is a spiritual process. It leads to self-responsibility. It leads to self-respect. It leads to self-esteem.

Self-Esteem: Foundations for Growth

Definitions of self-esteem focus on accepting one's self. Whether it means to know yourself, to appreciate yourself, to believe in yourself, or to hold a favorable opinion of yourself, people of high self-esteem like themselves. While they might be able to name things about themselves that they would like to change, they regard themselves overall with value and respect.

People with a high sense of self build their lives on certain principles and foundations. I call them foundations because I see them as the building blocks that help shape the way we build our lives. I have condensed them into the following four precepts.

1. People who have high self-esteem operate out of a sense of reality rather than fantasy. They accept their places within this reality and are keenly aware not only of their external situations but also of their internal feelings and knowledge.

2. People who operate with high self-esteem know how to alter their reality favorably through goals and purposes for their lives. They are able to set goals that are realistic and establish plans and strategies whereby the goals can be achieved.

3. People with high regard for themselves are able to set themselves apart from others. They are willing to stand up for themselves. They establish boundaries so that others do not infringe on their time, resources, energy, and physical being without express consent. This does not mean that they are cold and standoffish. They see themselves as integrally connected to but still separate from others.

4. People who appreciate themselves live their lives with integrity. Their ideals and their behaviors reflect each other. Their lives are integrated; their goals, their reality, their ideals, their behaviors, all operate out of a sense of self-knowledge. They strive for high standards.

None of these foundations occur in and of themselves. With determined effort to live in awareness, set goals and standards, establish personal boundaries, and live under a set of moral principles, self-esteem can be developed. It is, however, a conscious choice and one that takes effort.

A sentence beginning with the phrase "I know that I should . . . but . . . " is a dead giveaway for a person who is not living consciously and with purpose.

The poem "Autobiography in Five Chapters" (see page 30) represents a microcosm of this process. At first, the person is not aware of her present reality. She does not see the hole in the street; she blames others when she falls in; she is stuck ("it takes forever to get out"); she feels hopeless and lost. She repeats her pattern. This time, even though she is now aware of the reality, she is in denial, pretending that she does not see the hole. Again, she refuses to accept her responsibility in repeating past mistakes.

In the third chapter, a major shift occurs. She still falls in the hole, but this time her "eyes are open" and she realizes that it is her fault. She gets out quickly and begins to make changes. At first, the change is minor—she walks around the hole.

Walking down another street in the fifth and final chapter represents an acceptance of her reality. She sets a new goal not to fall in the hole. She acts on the new goal. She establishes a new way of life not only to avoid the hole but to stop encountering it at all. This is the process that is needed for life change to take place.

While developing this concept, I asked a group to

name characteristic behaviors of those who do not have the four foundations of self-esteem. Sometimes it is easier to understand a concept in the negative than in the positive. The list evolved as they called out behaviors.

- « Denial
- « Forgetfulness or distorted memory
- « Negativism
- « Irresponsibility
- « Living in a fantasy world
- « Blaming others
- « Ethical deterioration
- « Dependency
- « Confusion
- « Illusion of control
- « Dishonesty
- « Frozen or buried feelings

When I stepped back and looked at the easel carefully, I realized that we had just compiled a list of characteristics of addictive behavior patterns. Of course, low self-esteem is one of the chief attributes of an addictive person. People drink and use drugs in excess to fill a void.

This discovery made me realize how important building a good sense of self is. It is more than just feeling or saying, "I have high self-esteem." It is a matter of total emotional health. Working to develop good self-esteem means following the same principles as overcoming many emotional dependencies and addictions. Self-esteem is no longer just a segment of the "self-help" section in the bookstore. It is a healthy, whole way of living.

This list also helps identify those who appear to have high self-esteem but are hiding their real feelings.

Lynnette feels that she's right no matter what. She is constantly making mistakes, from spelling errors in letters to getting facts wrong at important meetings, but she either denies it or sees people who point these mistakes out as picky and obnoxious. Outwardly, she appears self-confident but, in fact, she is in denial, blames others, has an illusion of control, is dishonest, and lives in a fantasy world—all characteristics listed above as examples of low self-esteem. Her life is not integrated and whole.

The Spiritual Connection

If spirituality is a connectedness of the self to and with a vital force, a sense of self within a bigger picture, then self-esteem as a spiritual issue becomes more obvious. To live within a bigger picture is to live within one's physical reality and one's cosmic reality. It is making conscious choices to align one's life with the vital force in a positive way. It is knowing that this force is an integral part of one's being and is worth paying attention to. Living spiritually and with esteem means integrating both worlds in such a way that they intersect and function as one.

Foundations of Religion

The seventeenth-century Dutch philosopher Benedict de Spinoza is often credited with forming a Perennial Philosophy, which states that an infinite changeless reality exists at the core of every human being. Humankind's purpose is to discover this reality.[3]

Just as there are foundations for self-esteem, universal principles exist within all major world religions. I have named seven universals.

1. A universal "something" or presence exists that is named variously as Reality, Ultimate or Higher Power, Great Spirit, God, Goddess, or Mystery.

2. There is more to a human being than the body. An essential core of personality exists that is not physical and that is sometimes named the soul or spirit.

3. This core personality (soul) can unite with the universal presence during a lifetime.

4. The universal presence is found within all creatures, a principle known as the unity of life.

5. Reality is ultimately friendly; the universe is friendly and hopeful.

6. Life is made up of choices with cause-and-effect results.

7. There are certain principles for living that help lead to unity with the universal presence. Examples include the Golden Rule (do unto others as you would have them do to you), the Ten Commandments, Buddha's

Eightfold Path, Tao's The Way, and selfless service.

None of these universal principles of religion fall into the hierarchical, authoritarian models that so negatively affect self-esteem and spirituality. Here, instead, we find concepts of God that are both external as a force in the world and internal as a force within. Here we have a universe that is "friendly" rather than permeated with such a stench of sin that we must withdraw from the world in order to live a life of integrity. Here we find that we can be part of the whole, that we can unite with divinity and find joy rather than condemnation. Here women are equal with everyone.

The foundations of both self-esteem and spirituality speak about reality. Both speak about making choices in life. Most important, both speak to possibility—the possibility of a rich, fulfilling life ingrained in both concepts.

Choosing Not to Change

Coming into awareness is a powerful moment in one's life. Once you realize that something is "rotten in the state of Denmark," your life changes forever. For then you choose to live life differently or you choose to remain the same.

We all know (or are) people who continue to fall into holes in the sidewalk: women who repeat the pattern of going from one abusive or addictive relationship to another; bright, capable friends who end up in conflict with employer after employer; neighbors who say, "I know that I should quit smoking, lose weight, exercise regularly, but . . . "

What happens when these individuals (or we) realize the pattern? What is our response when we become aware that we need to change? For many, the response is to feel overwhelmed. The amount of work that it might take makes crawling back into bed, pulling the covers over our eyes, and going back to sleep seem like the most manageable approach. The catch is that, in the long run, it takes more energy to remain in denial than to change.

Betty sat thoughtfully in one of my workshops. Finally, she raised her hand. Her voice was slightly defensive as she spoke. "I can look at the sentence and say, 'I know that I should quit smoking, but . . . . But the reality is that I know that I'm not going to quit smoking even though I know that it's bad for me. So I don't want to change even though I'm aware."

At least Betty is aware and honest. What she might not realize is that it takes emotional energy to continue to act against her best interests. Now Betty must justify her actions to herself when she smokes, which interferes with her integrity. It takes emotional energy to ignore the facts and her inner voice. She has the freedom to make these decisions (thank heaven!). The one question that she needs to ask herself is, "Is the payoff that I get from smoking worth the energy depletion and betrayal of what I know to be best for me?"

Harriet dragged herself out of bed every Sunday morning. "I ought to raise my kids in church," was her often-repeated statement. Yet she came home each week feeling depressed.

"When I finally opened my ears and heard what the minister was saying each week, I didn't know what to do. I still believe that my kids need religious upbringing. But I kept hearing about this wonderful family ideal. Suddenly, I realized that we would never be like that. The children's father left three years ago. We just don't look like what the minister was describing. I know that I should look for a new church, but I don't know where to start."

As soon as Harriet heard the messages that she was receiving at church in addition to her own "I know I should, but . . . " statement, she decided to make a plan for change.

Harriet made arrangements for a church member to take her two children to the same church while she shopped around. That way, her children did not have to be dragged through several changes but could attend Sunday school each week. She finally settled on a new church that was more inclusive of different lifestyles. At first, the adjustment was difficult for the two children, but with time, they were happy in their new setting.

Determined to See

Healthy self-esteem calls for action, forcing us to act—to stand up and begin to make changes. Our spiritual centers tell us that we cannot rest until we have found peace within ourselves. Inner conflict stems from choosing not to do what needs to be done. Self-esteem and spirituality both require that we look down the street on which we walk and count the potholes.

Exercises: Counting Potholes

1. "I know that I should . . . but. . . ." Where in your life do you use this sentence? Make a list. Then prioritize the list. Which changes seem most important to make? Look at number one. What do you need to do first?

2. Did you identify with the list of behaviors that described addiction and nonawareness? If so, increase your knowledge by reading a book on addiction. Alcoholics Anonymous (AA) is listed in your phone directory and can give you the names of up-to-date resources. I like the writings of psychotherapist Anne Wilson Schaef, Ph.D. You also might want to talk to a professional in the field. Attending an AA meeting near you might also be helpful. Such meetings are nonthreatening, and the attendees never expect more of you than you can give.

3. Set two achievable goals for yourself for the next six months. Write down specific plans to attain them. Make sure that each step is small and can fit into your schedule. Don't say, "lose 30 pounds." Instead, make plans for each week: "I will eat reasonably and only at mealtime and will walk a half-hour each day." Allow yourself a day off to visit with friends or to lie on the couch reading a good book. Remember that a day of rest makes good sense (and it's scriptural).

4. Read over the list of universal principles of world religions. How do you feel about them? Make notes and share with a friend.

5. If you are totally overwhelmed in any area of your life, do not be afraid to go to a professional in that field or a counselor. This does not indicate weakness on your part. Instead, it means that you are serious about positive changes. Make that call if you feel that professional advice would be helpful.

4

Changing the Message

"My me is God."

—Saint Catherine of Genoa[1]

Living in Wisdom

She sits quietly on the floor, her back pressed firmly against the wall. Rays of early morning sun peek into the darkened room. The rest of the house is still. Slowly, her mind quiets. The day's agenda is silenced. Dishes, meetings, and children's soccer games will fall into place later. The first half-hour of the day is for listening.

Words from ancient wisdom, changed to reflect the feminine conscience, are recalled and slowly and voicelessly repeated within her mind.

She lives in wisdom who sees herself in all and all
    in her,
Whose love for the Lord of Love has consumed
Every selfish desire and sense-craving
    tormenting the heart.
Not agitated by grief nor hankering after
    pleasure,
She lives free from lust and fear and anger.
Established in meditation, she is truly wise.
Fettered no more by selfish attachments,
She is not elated by good fortune
Nor depressed by bad.
Such is the seer.[2]

By the time the woman rises from her half-hour routine of nurturing her inner self with positive passages and listening receptively, noises begin to fill the house. Showers run, the refrigerator door slams, the aroma of coffee leads her to the kitchen. She packs two school lunches, puts out cereal bowls and spoons for the children, and passes her husband in the hallway on the way to the now-empty shower. In the confusion and bustle that the rest of the day brings, does giving up extra sleep for contemplation make any difference?

"It took several months of beginning each day this way," Marcia says. "At first, I was tired. I had trouble remembering new passages. But then the routine settled in and my mind quieted down. Now I do see a difference. No lights have gone on; no bells have clanged. I'm just calmer. There have been no miracles. No lottery win to pay off the car and house. The bills are still there. I just don't fret over them so much. They always do get paid. . . ."

"I listen better. And I'm less insecure. I am able to see where someone else is coming from instead of becoming defensive about myself. In fact, my concentration at work has improved, so I'm more productive. Just as I've learned to shut out distractions in the morning during my meditation, I use that skill to shut out distractions at work. It's a nice change. Probably no one else notices, but I feel better." Marcia was thoughtful. "I like myself better this way," she added.

Messages Within

External as well as internal messages are absorbed into the psyche. The impact of media on self-image is now well-documented. Children who continually watch episodes of violence learn that violence is an acceptable means of dealing with problems. Advertisers convince viewers that their products are superior. Thin bodies of models become the accepted norm for women. Messages seen and heard often enough become part of our subconscious and conscious.

Child psychologists have found that young children absorb statements about who they are from their parents far more than they absorb messages about behavior. "You are lazy" sinks in more than "Brush you teeth before going to bed." "You are a bad person" will impact a child long after "Say thank you to Uncle Joe" has been obeyed.

Fortunately, many children also internalize positive messages: "You are good. You are worthy."

As your internal messages change, so does your self-esteem. It is time to reverse negative messages received in childhood from your parents, your teachers, and your peers. It is time to give up your need for external approval and discover your own infinite worth. It is time to let God fill you with wisdom and love.

The poverty of our society's internal strength is apparent when contrasted with other cultures. In 1990, the Dalai Lama did not understand when a Western psychologist spoke of low self-esteem. Even though he speaks English fluently, the phrase had to be translated several times into Tibetan for him to even grasp the notion. He was saddened to learn that so many people in America carry deep feelings of self-loathing and inferiority.

Although Tibetans suffer from severe oppression, were driven from their homeland, and watched their temples burned and fellow countrymen murdered, they do not suffer from low self-esteem.[3] When asked in another interview about his lack of anger toward the Chinese at the time he was awarded the Nobel Peace Prize, the Dalai Lama replied. "They have taken everything from us; should I let them take my mind as well?"[4]

One of the main tenets of meditation is that we become what we meditate on, or as poet Ralph Waldo Emerson said, "We are what we think about all day long." Thinking positive thoughts makes us positive people. Meditating on eternal truths helps us live by eternal truths. Hearing our inner voice helps us trust that voice. Constant practice means that no one can take our minds and souls as well.

Delving Down and Within

When my husband and I broke ground to build our new home in the mountains, we worked with an excavator to determine the exact location and siting of the house. In the process, we discussed the well that would be needed to provide water. We had heard with dismay about another family in the area who had drilled 500 feet and still had not reached water. Max, the excavator, nodded his head to one side and said with confidence, "You won't have any trouble. I can smell water right there. You'll have it at 60 feet." We drove a stake into the ground. Several weeks later the well driller came and said to us, "If Max said that this is the place, don't move the stake." Tom, the well driller, hit water at 50 feet. It wasn't a sufficient flow to provide water for the house. He had to go down farther for that. But the location was exact.

Years of working on projects such as ours have changed how Max relates to the earth. Years of practice have brought him so in tune with the earth that he is able to locate water in a fashion that totally astounded my husband and me.

The Christian scriptures contain a story about water. Jesus asks a woman to draw water from a well and give him a drink. As they talk, Jesus speaks about "living water." He says, "But those who drink of the water that I give them will never be thirsty. The water that I will give will become in them a spring of water gushing up to eternal life" (John 4:14).

Max was able to find water in the ground through his training and his close relationship to the earth. We can train ourselves to find "living water" within.

Elsewhere Jesus said, "The kingdom of God is within you" (Luke 17:21).

Swami Ramdas, a nineteenth-century Hindu mystic wrote, "Forget not the central truth, that God is seated in your own heart."[5]

Kabir, a Muslim, wrote in the fifteenth century, "The Lord is in me, the Lord is in you, as life is in every seed."[6]

The resurgent Goddess movement has very little in the way of written documents. However, in the Charge of the Goddess, a major part of Goddess spirituality rituals, are found these words: "If that which you seek you find not within yourself, you shall never find it without."[7]

SELF AND SOUL

The tradition does not matter. One of the universal precepts of all religions is the indwelling of the divine within each person. Making oneself available to the messages from this spiritual center is the premise upon which meditation is built and the means to change our internal messages and enhance our self-worth.

Not Just the Mind

Physical benefits of meditation are well-documented. In *The Relaxation Response*, Herbert Benson, M.D., confirms studies that report that ill people who engage in regular meditation heal faster than those who do not. The body consumes less oxygen during meditation, blood pressure drops in those with elevated pressures, and heart rate decreases.[8] A 1978 study found that people who practiced the transcendental meditation technique regularly for fewer than 5 years had an average biological age 5 years younger than their chronological ages. More significant, however, was that those who had been meditating longer than 5 years had an average biological age 12 years younger than their chronological ages.[9]

Those who cease meditating lose the benefits of the practice almost immediately. A Hindu saying tells that one day lost in meditation requires seven to make it up.

The Buddha, saying that he had not gained anything through meditation, was then asked what good it is. He replied, "Let me tell you what I lost through meditation: sickness, anger, depression, insecurity, the burden of old age, the fear of death. That is the good of meditation."[10]

The Practice of Meditation

If you read 15 different books on meditation, you will undoubtedly read 15 different methods to use in meditation. The essential element in all of them, however, is to still the constant movement of the mind and open oneself to deeper insights. It is a training process—training the mind to detach from worldly cares. Eventually, as the Dalai Lama said, no one will be able to take or control your mind.

By focusing on something other than the thoughts that usually race unchecked through the mind, the thinking process can be halted. It is being in the present moment without other concerns. When thoughts come barging into the process, whether it be today's long to-do list, the insult Aunt Mabel hurled yesterday evening, or your mother's terminal illness, you can simply set aside these concerns.

The important thing in meditation is to learn what works for you. You can spend hundreds of dollars and attend a meditation retreat to learn one particular method. Or you can experiment at home, listen to your body, and find your own style.

Here are suggestions to get you started.

❨ Early morning is usually recommended for several reasons. The house or apartment is quiet. If you live alone, noise may not be a problem, especially since the telephone usually does not ring at 6:30 A.M.

Early morning is also desirable because you are more likely to be consistent in your practice. It is too easy to say, "I'm tired. I need a hot bath to relax. I'll do it tomorrow" after a long workday. It is also easier to meditate before your mind has been churned up with other concerns.

❨ Decide how much time is best for you. Thirty minutes is considered the optimal amount of time for meditation. However, something is better than nothing. If you have only 15 minutes, by all means, try to utilize these 15 minutes. Don't say, "I don't have a half-hour; therefore, I can't meditate." Perhaps you will also be able to add another 15-minute block later in the day.

❨ Next, find a comfortable position. Some people sit in a chair; others sit on the floor with legs crossed lotus-style. You do not need to do flexibility exercises or twist your body in some yoga-style pose to meditate. What is important is to sit with your back straight. This allows maximum blood and oxygen flow to the brain. You may want to sit with your back against a wall. If you sit in a chair, keep your feet on the floor. This will help keep your back straight.

☾ Most people let their hands lie in their laps. Some clasp their hands together lightly. Others rest their hands so that their palms are facing upward, in a receptive manner.

What is important is that you find a position and stick with it. Eventually, just placing your body in this pose in the same quiet room at the same time of day will trigger the response of quieting the mind. Consistency is vital.

☾ Choose a point of focus to quiet your mind. Listed below are five common methods. Remember that none of these are sacrosanct. They are merely tools to help quiet your mind. Again, the important thing is to decide which will work best for you, and after experimenting to determine this, stick to your choice.

Points of Focus

1. Following the breath. As you sit in the quiet, notice your breathing. Inhale and exhale in a rhythmic pattern, a little slower than normal. Concentrate on your breathing. As you focus on your breath, fewer thoughts will invade your mind. If your mind wanders from your breathing, quietly bring it back to the breath. With practice and repetition, your mind will clear with less concentration on your breathing. The Hebrew word *ruah* means both "breath" and "spirit." Focusing on your breath is an appropriate way to be in touch with your spirit.

2. The mantra. Repetition of a significant word or phrase, when repeated in meditation, also focuses the mind. I recommend the name of a divine being that is significant to you. For Christians it might be Jesus or the prayer, "Jesus Christ, son of God, have mercy." Hindus might find Rama or Krishna meaningful; those with a Jewish background, the Shema ("Hear O Israel, the Lord our God is one") or Baruch attah Adonai ("Blessed art thou, O Lord"); Muslims might use "Allah" or "God is one, the Eternal God."

Repetition of the holy name is especially useful for those devout in their faiths. If you felt injured or slighted by your childhood faith, it is best to avoid this method, unless you are intentionally trying to heal those wounds.

The principle is the same as with the breath. Quietly or silently repeat your chosen mantra during your time of meditation. Do not be tempted to think about the divinity that you have chosen and his or her good qualities, or how you wish you could live your life according to his or her precepts. Just keep repeating the holy name. When other thoughts come to your mind, let them pass and return to your mantra.

The mantra can also be repeated quietly to the self throughout the day while performing chores or taking a walk. It keeps you in tune with your divine center and brings a holy force into your life.

Catholics have used mantras for years with the assistance of the rosary. Use of a mantra is the basis for transcendental meditation.

3. An image. Staring at an object or image during meditation suits some people well. Focusing on a sacred object, such as a seated Buddha or a crucifix or cross, can work if you can resist interpreting that image to yourself during the quiet time. A bowl of fresh flowers or some memento of significance in your life could also serve this purpose.

4. Candle gazing. A candle flame is a commonly used object for meditation. Stare into the candle until the image of the flame is clearly implanted in your mind. Close your eyes. You should be able to retain the image of the flame even with your eyes closed. If you lose the image, open your eyes and stare into the flame again. I know many people who prefer this method. It quiets the rumblings of their thoughts.

To use this technique most effectively, place the candle at eye level in a darkened, draft-free room.

5. Passage memorization. This is the type of meditation described at the beginning of this chapter. It involves memorizing passages of positive spiritual value and repeating them slowly and silently to yourself during your meditation time.[11] It does not mean thinking about the passages or evaluating them—just entering them into your subconscious and keeping your mind free during the process.

The passage used in this chapter (on page 44) is the opening verse of the second chapter of the Bhagavad Gita, the chapter that Mahatma Gandhi used daily during his meditation. The *he's* in the passage have been changed to *she's* so that Marcia can relate to it better.

This method requires the additional discipline of memorization. However, it provides an added benefit of a repertoire of passages committed to memory over a period of time—passages of wisdom that can help direct your life and inspire you during difficult times.

This is the method that I have come to find most useful. I believe that just as television scripts can affect our well-being, so can constant feeding of positive words from ancient scriptures. I do not limit myself to one tradition but pull from many traditions—Christian, Hindu, Buddhist, Native American. My criteria are that they are positive and something to which I aspire. Several books are now on the market with readings from various religions. I recommend *God Makes the Rivers to Flow*, compiled by Eknath Easwaran.

Final Thoughts

When you come out of your meditation, sit quietly and refocus to your environment. If you are used to active prayer, this is a good time to say a short prayer. Remember, however, that active prayer differs from meditation. Prayer is a communication process whereby you think about what you say. Meditation provides the opportunity to be receptive to answers.

Remember also that the goal of meditation is not to see lights or visions or to hear voices. It is to still your mind. It is not positive thinking—we are not thinking during meditation. We are just being. Do not look for results. The process is enough. Anything else that comes is a gift. With time you may be able to look at all thoughts and banish them as you do in meditation—negative thoughts about yourself, messages from a wounded childhood. You will see them for what they are—thoughts, not reality.

Exercise: Meditation

Select one of the methods of meditation. Decide on the time of day, how much time you will devote, your position, and your focus. Practice for one month. What difference has it made in you? Try to make this a daily habit.

5

Our Bodies, Our Souls

"Do not disdain your body. For your soul is just as safe in the body as in the Kingdom of heaven."

—Mechtild of Magdeburg, thirteenth century[1]

The Impossible, Unhealthy Ideal

If acceptance of oneself is a key factor in self-esteem, it is no wonder that women have low ratings. Women consistently have trouble accepting the most visible part of themselves—their bodies. One Gallup poll showed that 98 percent of American women would like to change something about their physical selves. American women have more negative images about their bodies than women from any other country.

Body fixation is a factor that cannot be ignored in our culture. Intellectually, most women will concur that this obsession is out of control. Yet, they also admit that emotionally, it affects them.

The current ideal for women is a young White blond, very thin, with long legs and an ample bosom, even though the average woman is five feet four inches tall and weighs 143 pounds. Over half of all American women wear size 14 or larger, yet most stores stock sizes 6 to 10 far more (and have a more fashionable selection) than they do the larger sizes.

A basic list of "body facts" drawn from various sources highlights this absurdity.

❝ Ninety percent of obesity studies are conducted on women, even though there are more overweight men.

❝ A 1992 study showed that 27.7 percent of White female teenagers smoke, compared to 5.9 percent of Black female teenagers. A key reason is weight. Black culture permits women to be heavier and still be attractive.[2]

❝ At any one time, half of the nine-year-old girls in this country are dieting.

❝ Americans spend $10 billion each year on diet aids and strategies, 95 percent of which have proven ineffective over a five-year span.

« When women were not assertive, heavier bodies were in style (for example, the 1950s). During periods of history when women became more independent, the fashion industry created a thinner, wasted-away, little-girl look. In the 1920s, after women received the right to vote, the linear form replaced the curvaceous.[3]

« Finnish researchers in Helsinki studied department store mannequins from the 1920s to the 1990s and, through measurements, worked out theoretical body fat. Mannequins resembled average women's shapes until the 1950s, when they started to become thinner. A young adult woman today averages 37-inch hips; mannequins are down to 31-inch hips. "Women as thin as these mannequins would probably not menstruate, since it is thought that women need a certain minimum percentage of body fat in order to menstruate."[4]

« Models, who resemble these mannequins (or do the mannequins resemble the models?) weigh 23 percent less than the average American woman weighs. The definition of semistarvation is 25 percent weight loss. During food rationing that took place during in World War II in parts of Europe, extra food was given to people who dropped 25 percent of their weight. Perhaps it is time to provide extra food to models and young girls who try to emulate them.

« During the Victorian era, corsets often resulted in broken ribs. The current obsession with a "perfect" figure has led to severe illness and even death for thousands of young women who starve themselves to thinness. Anorexia nervosa and bulimia, the extremes of eating disorders, send major signals that this fixation has gone too far.

❧ Women undergo face-lifts, liposuction, breast implants, and other mutilations to their bodies pursuing the look of endless youth and beauty. I know of one 21-year-old who spent an entire inheritance from her grandfather on liposuction for her hips and stomach.

These facts, which have been in the national consciousness for a long time, bombard us, in spite of evidence that being underweight or overly thin is as unnatural and unhealthy as being greatly overweight.

Because body size is an emotional issue, it is often difficult to change behaviors through rational dialogue. As stated earlier, most women, when asked, know that the current standard is not natural. Yet they strive to achieve it. Melinda, who is five feet ten inches tall and wears a size six, said, "I now know not to trust my own judgment when I look in the mirror. Even though I was skinny, my father always called me fat when he wanted to upset me. I still think that I am fat. Now my husband helps me determine if I've gained or lost too much weight. Without his help I would always think that I needed to lose more."

Or, as noted feminist and founder of *Ms.* magazine, Gloria Steinem, wrote, "In my own mind, I am still that fat brunette from Toledo, and I always will be."[5]

The Disconnected Body

Women have learned to disconnect themselves from their bodies. Survivors of incest and rape use disconnection as an emotional safe haven from their past experiences. Some survivors utilize unpopular body images to prevent further attacks. One very overweight woman said, "My fat protects me. Men no longer look at me as a sex object. You can criticize my weight, but it serves me well."

Author Candy Zulkosky relayed the following to me when I was sharing these findings with her: "I knew a nurse/psychology instructor who had been raped. She once told me that she decided, in an unconscious decision, that she would become fat after the rape. Then no man would ever want her again. She knew it. She succeeded. And regretted the decision because time helped heal the wounds of rape, but she was stuck in a body that she despised as much as she hated the rapist."

A certain disconnection happens for most women just because the currently idealized body is so far from reach and because our society emphasizes the female body so erotically. To remember that the main function of the breast is to provide milk for babies is to go up against all popular concepts of female anatomy as an instrument of pleasure for men.

Equally harmful is the denigration of the body set forth by the Western church. The body is seen as the seat of sin where the senses inflame the passions and the female body leads to the downfall of the male's soul. The Christian church is not the only religious group with such teachings. Muslims drape their women in black with only their eyes visible. To reveal an ankle is sinful because it may lead a man to passion.

On one hand, society's norm says that without bodies, women are nothing. On the other hand, religious teachings imply that because of their bodies, women are nothing. No matter how it is viewed, women end up as nothing.

Cultural traditions in parts of the Middle East, Africa, Indonesia, and Malaysia allow for female genital mutilation of young girls. Their bodies are sacrificed for a cultural religious norm, which also keeps them "pure" until marriage. In Myanmar (formerly Burma), some women wear 15 to 20 necklaces. These are designed so that the necklaces hold up their necks, but eventually the neck muscles atrophy. If a woman is disobedient, a few necklaces can be removed, resulting in excruciating pain from trying to keep her head up. The Chinese broke the feet of women and forced their toes back. Tiny feet were considered the ideal of beauty, but, in fact, this was a practice that prevented a woman from ever getting away. Other cultures have put heavy ankle bracelets on the legs of women, which destroy the muscles of the leg in a fashion similar to the necklaces of Myanmar. Over time, each of these practices has evolved into a symbol of beauty:

necklaces, ankle bracelets, small feet, and for Western White women today, thinness as a result of semistarvation.

Studies show that people given the small number of calories needed to maintain the low body weights popular today cannot function well. Even mental acuity suffers. Another dangerous possibility is kidney and other organ malfunction, which can lead to permanent internal damage and possibly death. In the extreme, the disconnection of the body from life is total.

The Body and Self-Esteem

The body is an integral part of who we are and how we view ourselves. It is definitely related to self-esteem. Women who have accepted their bodies have higher self-esteem than those who haven't. They can feel sexy (that is, feel attractive) and project that self-confidence, without compromising themselves. They are able to love themselves, body and soul.

For a woman to affirm her body as life-giving and an important part of who she is requires another disconnection—a disconnection from the beauty mystique of her culture.

A healthy body feeds the mind and soul, just as an unhealthy, emaciated body cripples it. Generally, people know what to do to maintain healthy bodies. They know to eat properly, to exercise regularly, to get at least seven hours of sleep per night, and to avoid toxins such as cigarette smoke and drugs.

Even though these principles of good health are taught and acknowledged, American culture does not promote them. Advertisers bombard the psyche with cigarettes and alcohol; with high-fat and high-salt snacks; with high-heeled, narrow-toed shoes that cripple the feet; with the "good life" as one of being waited upon rather than one of physical activity. Even sleep deprivation is applauded. People who say, "Gee, I went to bed at 10:00 last night," are yawned at; those who talk about staying up until 2:00 A.M. to finish reports for work are not only venerated but also promoted. We have bought the myth that the busier we are, the more important we are.

Once again, studies have shown that this lifestyle is destructive not only to the body but also to the soul. People who exercise regularly have a higher sense of self-esteem. Not only that but also the spiritual is strongly connected to the body. Individuals who exercise regularly have been found to be more open to spiritual experiences.[6]

Self-care of the body directly impacts self-care of the self and soul.

Learning to Count

Women learn to count calories. My friend Susan can tell you how many calories are in just about any food, from a cola drink to a fish fillet to a baked potato with butter. Ten years ago, I began counting grams of fat when the relationship of fat to cholesterol and body weight began to be more widely known. The same tablespoon of butter that represented 101 calories to Susan tallied up to 12 grams of fat for me. The same restrictive thinking applied—only the devil's name was changed.

Today I count neither calories nor fat. My system is much more positive. How many fruits and vegetables can I eat in one day, with the minimum number being five? The norm now set by the American Medical Association is to consume five to nine servings of fruits and vegetables each day. Just eating fresh wholesome food makes me more conscious of good eating habits. That awareness helps keep junk food out of the house and piles of apples, bananas, broccoli, and spinach in the kitchen. The reality that I need to eat two vegetables or fruits per meal means that my breakfast will consist mostly of fruit, not fruit-flavored cereal.

You wouldn't buy a $30,000 car and proceed to pour kerosene into it and expect it to run for 100,000 miles. You would purchase the level octane gasoline recommended by the manufacturer, change the oil regularly, rotate the tires as needed, and wash off accumulated salt and cinders after a winter storm.

Why, then, do people ply themselves with doughnuts and pastries, drink caffeine-laden coffee and soda, inhale tobacco, ingest drugs, expose the body to constant stress, never recharge the batteries through aerobic exercise, and then wonder why their bodies begin to give out after 45 years? Instead of acknowledging that they had a part in rusting out their own vehicles, they look to medicine and miracle cures.

Think of food as fuel for the body. This does not mean that we should eat in isolation rather than with our families or that a feast is not a meal to share with important people in our lives. This does not mean that we cannot enjoy a piece of cake on our birthdays. What it does mean is that we must give our bodies the nutrients that they need as efficient fuel to run smoothly. That fuel comes from wholesome fruits, vegetables, and whole-grain products.

Another effective analogy is the scriptural mandate that the body is the temple of God. If someone came into your church, mosque, ashram, or synagogue and threw mud around, how would you feel? Why, then, do we throw mud into our own temples?

The quote by the thirteenth-century Christian mystic, Mechtild of Magdeburg, that began this chapter provides a positive image of the body as the housing for the soul. The Hindu hymn "The Real Lovers of God" by Narsinha Mehta reads, "Their bodies are like sacred shrines in which the Lord of Love is seen."[7] Saint Paul wrote, "Your body is a temple of the Holy Spirit within you" (I Corinthians 6:19). Even though much religious practice has disconnected the body from the soul, mystics of every religion have kept the two closely tied together.

Saint Francis of Assisi called his body his donkey, which carried his soul around the countryside so that he could be of service.

Howard J. Clinebell, Jr., offers the following in his book, *Well Being*: "A body that's as alive and fit as possible provides a strong foundation for your overall wholeness, including your spiritual wholeness." He suggests thinking of the body from a holistic, spiritual perspective to help motivate people to better self-care. "If you've been treating your body carelessly or shabbily, establishing a loving reconnection with it via better self-care can be a kind of spiritual rebirth."[8]

The Animal Question

As a committed vegetarian, I am in good company with Socrates; Benjamin Franklin; John Wesley; Henry David Thoreau; Thomas Jefferson; Mahatma Gandhi; Peace Pilgrim; and several million Buddhists, Hindus, and Seventh-Day Adventists.

The biological approach to vegetarianism says that my body was made to process whole, living foods—fruits, vegetables, whole grains, nuts. My intestinal tract is long— 12 times the length of my trunk, like herbivores', such as cows. My dog's intestine is only 3 times the length of her trunk. That means that meat does not spend a long time in her body. As a carnivore, her stomach produces 10 times the amount of hydrochloric acid that mine does. This rapidly breaks down meat and sends it out of her system quickly.

A human body, however, has no such system. The stomach does not produce the acid necessary to fully break down meat (which includes red meat, chicken, and fish). The longer trip through the intestinal track means that animal flesh has begun decaying before it is finally eliminated, leaving toxic waste in the body. While our livers have the capability of eliminating only small amounts of uric acid, the main acid released in meat consumption, the carnivore's liver can eliminate 10 to 15 times more.

The spiritual issue of vegetarianism draws from the list of the principles of world religion. The universal presence is found within all creatures. All creatures are sacred. To kill any, even for the purpose of food, is to violate universal law.

These two approaches to vegetarianism converge when studies of health are conducted on religious groups that adhere to a meatless diet. A study of 35,460 Seventh-Day Adventists living in California showed that Adventists live, on average, seven years longer than the general population. Seventy percent fewer Adventists die from cancer, 68 percent fewer from respiratory diseases, 60 percent fewer from heart disease, and 46 percent fewer from strokes than the general California population.

A more careful analysis of this population showed that Adventists who did get heart disease or bowel cancer ate more fish, meat, and dairy products than other Seventh-Day Adventists. Those Adventists who did not get cancer were reported to have eaten more fruits and vegetables.[9]

T. Colin Campbell of Cornell University in Ithaca, New York, confirmed these findings in a study of various Chinese populations, which compared those segments of China that were vegetarian with those that were meat-eating.[10]

American society is such a meat-based culture that it is difficult for many people to comprehend a life without chicken and beef. The "P" word, protein, is usually raised as a defense, even though it is well-documented that Americans eat too much protein and that adequate amounts of protein can be derived from plant sources.

I know it works for me. I have far more energy since I stopped eating animal products. Not only that, but I never have to worry about my weight. It has remained constant for the past 15 years. I do not have to count fat—most fat is found in meat and dairy products, which I do not consume. I do not feel sluggish. And I feel more alive and well, knowing that other creatures are not being sacrificed for me to eat.

I spent many years as a vegetarian before the spiritual implications of it came home for me. The process was long because I focused on health rather than total well-being. Today I feel more connected to all living creatures. I feel, because of my self-care, more connected to the universe.

Changing Course

New habits are hard. It takes two to three months of a new lifestyle habit before you can consider it permanent in your life. Start small.

❝ Add more fruits and vegetables.

❝ Walk 20 minutes a day.

❝ Have beans and rice for dinner once a week.

Slowly you will feel the difference.

Exercise does wonders in relieving stress, reducing anger, and eliminating other negative emotions that may plague you. The chemicals that are stimulated in the brain through aerobic exercise are effective in controlling mild depression.

Be realistic. Sally is a 37-year-old professional woman with flexible work hours. She noted that when she attended aerobic classes with 23-year-old young professionals, the vast difference in age did not help her self-esteem. The exercise program only reminded her of her lack of tone and conditioning. When she was able to go to the class where middle-age women were the main attendees, she could enjoy the exercise more and was able to maintain the program because she felt better about herself there.

Learn to love your body. Appreciate it as it is. Make a commitment to it as you would to something or someone you truly value. Treat yourself to a massage or a leisurely bubble bath. Enjoy the pleasures of sex and the sensual experiences.

Try valuing the messages from other bodily senses. Take time to smell the roses, to listen to the birds or your favorite symphony, to taste a new fruit that you have never tried before.

Listen to your body. It will tell you when to say no, when to rest, and when to move forward. It will give you messages about your world.

When you finally get to the point where you love your body and treat it appropriately, you will no longer obsess about it. In fact, it will be so much a part of you that you will forget about it. It will be *your* body—your healthy, loving body, the temple that it is.

Exercises: Bodywork

1. For one month, eat five to nine fruits and vegetables daily. Note how this changes other eating habits. What do you eliminate just because you are too full?

2. Begin a sensible exercise program three to five times per week. It will be easier if you enlist a friend with similar goals. Walking with a buddy helps motivation. You may initially feel tired. What happens after the third week? What new energy do you have?

3. After one month of exercises 1 and 2, note any difference in how you feel, not just physically but emotionally. What new insights have you gained? Compare notes with your exercise buddy.

6

Beyond the Self: Finding the Unity of All Life

"For hatred can never put an end to hatred; love alone can. This is an unalterable law."

—Buddha[1]

The Goal of Inner Peace

Imagine that you have achieved an inner peace so complete that you finally have no question about your self-worth. You are so comfortable and in tune with your inner essence that none of the old haunting questions arise. Never again do you wonder if you are worthy of someone else's approval. No more do you ask, "Can I do it?" The questions about what others think have long ago left your consciousness. You are at home with yourself. The issue of self-esteem becomes irrelevant.

Being totally at home with yourself means being in concert with the divine that exists both within and outside you. Now *your* inner voice, not others' opinions and desires for you, guides you. You have complete confidence in that voice.

You have learned inner calm through meditative practices. Your body is in tune with your soul. Your healthful practices have led to a new sense of well-being. You have made positive and uplifting choices in all phases of your life, from beneficial habits to inspirational thoughts. You listen to yourself. Negative, critical thinking is nowhere to be found.

Can you make this dream become a reality?

Change and Growth

"It was a transformative experience." Janelle spoke in a hushed voice to the five women who gathered for the weekend. "I took to heart the suggestions of trying these different exercises. It was hard at first because I kept trying to find support from others. But they just wanted their breakfast at the same time each day. They said nice things about my meditation, but I could tell that it was only because they thought they should. And when I announced that after work I was going to take a walk rather than help with homework or mend clothes or start dinner immediately, well, I thought I was going to have a Boston Tea Party on my hands!" Janelle laughed at herself at this point. Her eyes sparkled as she reflected on her boldness with her family.

Janelle is a loan officer at a bank. Her job requires that she balance the regulations of the bank and people's need for money. The tension between the two can be exhausting. At home, Janelle has three school-age children and a truck driver husband who is often away for several days at a time. She has to juggle a great deal to accomplish everything that needs to be done.

"Work was only a problem at lunchtime or other eating occasions when I began to decline food offerings. We have one secretary who actually feels insulted if you don't take one of her homemade goodies. I began to realize that that was her self-esteem problem and not mine.

"Anyway, I do feel much better, but not just physically. Totally. And the things that I was told would happen did," says Janelle.

Janelle's changes occurred when she declared herself in charge of her inner and outer life. Some old friends fell away. Highly energized, optimistic people came into her life and filled the gaps.

"We do attract what we are. You know, I think the

hardest thing about making these important changes was not me. It was other people. I cannot believe how much internal energy is consumed resisting other's negative vibes."

The path of least resistance is to do nothing and make no changes. However, if you want to grow and change like Janelle did, you must make choices and take action.

"At first, I was angry with my family. Of course, they hadn't said anything, but their foot dragging basically told me that they were putting up with my new life but would sure be glad when I got off this kick and went back to my old ways.

"I got so distracted that I never got to the transformative part." Janelle switched her dialogue from talking about others' reactions to her own changes.

"Without realizing it, I began to look at other people differently. Slowly, I realized that instead of anger, I felt sorry for them. Not sorry like pity. It is just that I began to see that everyone would like to have an inner strength like I was finding. Everyone wants good in their lives. They've just been taught as I had—that to be happy you need people who affirm you and meet your needs. I certainly believed that. How could I be angry at people who were just doing what I had done for years? Think of the folks who must have been frustrated with me when they made life changes and I didn't understand."

Self-responsibility is a principle of self-esteem. People who take responsibility for their personal growth experience higher self-esteem than those who do not. Janelle is experiencing higher self-esteem since she began to put suggestions for improving her physical and spiritual well-being into practice.

"Now that I'm over the hump, I actually feel more connected to my family and co-workers than before. I know that they have the same desires that I do. I look at my job in a new way, although probably no one sees any difference. I really try to do the best for each customer, knowing that this loan is important to them. At the same time, I am aware that by protecting the interest requirements of the bank, more funds will be available to other customers later. I see my job as a partnership role rather than the adversarial role it had been before. I'm beginning to feel connected to the world at large, too."

All of creation is bound together by this oneness, which most people call God. Janelle has begun to experience the oneness of all creation. It begins by understanding similarities rather than differences between people. That awareness grows into a consciousness that the divine lives in others and connects to the divine within us. Finally, the sense of oneness with God moves beyond humanity to a oneness with all of creation.

Mystics share this confirmation of the unity of life. They have revelations or spiritual experiences that validate this belief. They affirm a universal bonding that alters how they view all other people and creatures. I find their stories very instructive.

Once you understand and believe that the same core exists in everyone and everything, you realize that hurting another person or creature hurts you. The destructiveness of adversarial relationships becomes more apparent. The love felt within is transformed to love for all fellow creatures.

Stumbling Blocks to Living Fully

The Hindu scripture, the Bhagavad Gita, says that there are three gates into the house of sorrow: fear, anger, and greed. These are relational emotions. You are afraid of someone or something, angry at someone or some situation, or greedy or desirous for something.

Yet, these emotions all state something about your very core—how you feel about yourself in relation to something or someone else. Religious systems talk about fear, anger, and greed negatively. Religion teaches that these emotions are destructive to the person who harbors them. They keep you stuck in your present stage of growth. They eat away at you.

Fear

When my husband and I bought a home in Philadelphia in 1990, one of the first things John did was go around the house and rip out the wires for the security system. "I am not going to live in fear," he said, "worrying if some wire is tripped or some alarm rings."

We were not careless. We locked our doors. The dog barked at strangers. We did not own most things burglars looked for anyway, having removed television and expensive gadgets from our lives. The trappings of a security system—which, in reality, is an insecurity system—were more than we wanted in our lives.

There is a wonderful story about a town that was immobilized by a dragon that lived on the mountain and bellowed forth smoke and roared thunderous growls. The townspeople were too paralyzed by their fear of the dragon to go anywhere.

Finally, a little girl decided that she would not be intimidated by the fear that gripped her neighbors, and she started out to climb the mountain amidst discouraging remarks and warnings. Her ascent up the mountain was met with roars and belching smoke. As she climbed, however, she noticed the huge dragon getting smaller. On and on she climbed. When she finally reached the dragon's cave, she found that she could pick him up and place him in her small hand.

Going into and through our fears is the best way to overcome them. It is in standing and talking in front of a group that we learn that we do not have to be afraid of a large number of people. It is in applying for a new job that we learn that we do not need to do the same work for a lifetime. It is in ending a destructive relationship that we learn we can live on our own. It is in doing what we fear will bring dire consequences that we learn the consequences are never as severe as our fear of them. We learn that we do have the inner resources that we were afraid were lacking. We learn what scriptures of all faiths tell us, "Do not be afraid."

Diminishing fear means developing more trust in ourselves to handle life. Diminishing fear automatically means increasing self-esteem, because handling life with confidence is esteeming oneself.

Women are taught to fear from childhood up. They are trained to be afraid to go out at night. They are taught to be afraid of strangers, even though the majority of abuse is inflicted by family members and people known to them. They learn that many activities that boys consider normal and fun should be avoided by girls because of some unspecified fear.

When I was out hiking by myself last year, I fell and hurt my leg. I knew that I could not finish the last eight miles in the mountains with my injury. Fortunately, I was close to a dirt road and came upon a car with a man in it who was glad to drive me to my pickup spot. When I relayed my story to friends, not one said, "How fortunate that you fell so near help." Their universal response was, "That could have been dangerous, getting a ride with a stranger." I felt that being injured in the woods alone was far more dangerous.

Many of us learned to fear because of abusive parents or neighborhood bullies. We learned to fear because children, from their own insecurities, made fun of others who did not act within peer boundaries. Fear of being different, of not matching up, and of being criticized or mocked controlled our lives. We did not understand that those causing the fear acted out of their own fears. Realizing the universal oneness of all people belies the myths that fear presents.

Because as young girls we did not learn to distinguish between self-imposed fear and true risk, we may end up making poor choices. There is a difference between walking down the streets of north Philadelphia or Los Angeles at 3:00 A.M. and being afraid to leave your suburban apartment by yourself at 5:00 P.M. You do not want to put yourself in danger. On the other hand, you do not want to live in constant fear and refuse challenges and opportunities for change and improvement in your life. You can live safely without fear.

You can also learn to understand what lies beneath the actions of those who hurt and maim you. People who hurt others obviously have not felt the warmth and love of the inner soul. They may think that they are more powerful and try to cause fear within others. Yet they are hurting themselves by injuring the unity of life that is within them.

When Cantor Michael Weisser and his wife, Julie, moved to their new home in Lincoln, Nebraska, in 1991, they were harassed by the Grand Dragon of the Ku Klux Klan, Larry Trapp. Trapp, a Nazi sympathizer, had terrorized African-American, Asian, and Jewish families in Nebraska and Iowa. The police warned the Weissers that Trapp made explosives and was dangerous. Trapp was planning to blow up the synagogue that Weisser had come to serve.

Julie Weisser decided that there was only one way to deal with the threat. Instead of living in fear, the Weissers approached Trapp and befriended him. By the time Trapp died from complications of diabetes 15 months later, he had converted to Judaism and renounced his association with the Klan.

The incredible story of Trapp's conversion is told in *Not by the Sword* by Kathryn Watterson. When the Weissers finally made contact with Trapp, they found a man who kept a Nazi flag and double-life-size picture of Hitler on a wall. He had assembled assault rifles, pistols, and shotguns. He had built a secret bunker for the coming "race wars." Against the advice of friends, Julie Weisser decided to reach out with kindness to the man whom, by all accounts, she should be fearing.

The dragon that she and her husband finally met was a man who had been regularly beaten and called a little queer by his father. He turned himself into a dragon of the Ku Klux Klan to bellow and roar and be feared by others in order to make himself feel bigger and more important. Like the dragon in the story above, Trapp was a gentle person looking for affection under his bravado.

If the Weissers had remained fearful, their fears might have proven true. Their synagogue would have been destroyed. They might have been harmed. By moving through their fear they gained a friend and watched this new friend's life gain meaning before he died.[2]

For women, overcoming fear means overcoming years of negative conditioning. Gerald Jampolsky under-scores this clearly in his book *Love Is Letting Go of Fear*.

Anger

Love is also letting go of anger, the second destructive gate to the house of sorrow. While women are taught to fear, they are simultaneously taught not to be angry. The difficulty for women in overcoming destructive anger is that our automatic response has become repression, which is also destructive.

Anger is a natural emotion, a response to being injured or rejected. Anger often comes in response to fear. If women are taught to be fearful, the incidence of anger increases. But when the secondary emotion of anger is sup-pressed, the amount of unexpressed anger grows inside.

Learning to identify how anger feels is the first step

to dealing with this emotion. Women are often afraid to feel anger. They assume that the only way to express it is violently, as they may have seen adults in their lives do. Yet naming anger can be transformative.

Identifying anger can be a catalyst for change. If someone is ignoring you or injuring you, anger can be the wake-up call that the relationship is out of sync and needs to be altered or terminated. Anger can lead you to call the Better Business Bureau about the lousy paint job by your contractor. Anger can move you to challenge your patronizing doctor or to begin the search for a physician who is more sympathetic to women's needs. As an instrument to force you to evaluate a part of your life, anger can be beneficial.

Anger can also be destructive. When anger is not dealt with in a healthy manner, it festers. Just imagine yourself angry. You can feel your blood pressure mount, a tension headache approaching, gastric juices churning in your stomach. If the anger sits within you, it can physically destroy you. There is a difference between being angry and becoming an angry person. Angry people never let go of their embitterment and dump it on others.

Warnings about anger in holy writings of many traditions stem from concern about its destructive nature. From the Christian admonition, "Be angry but do not sin; do not let the sun go down on your anger" (Colossians 4:26) to the Hindu, "Anger clouds the judgment; you no longer learn from past mistakes" (Bhagavad Gita, II, verse 63), warnings abound.

The advice seems contradictory: Learn to feel the emotion of anger but don't be angry. Healthy anger is a process. One feels angry but, rather than ignoring it, analyzes it and decides upon appropriate action. The action may indeed be to do nothing, but that is now a choice and not a reflexive denial.

Approaching anger with the same courage as facing fear is beneficial. It is by entering the anger that you can move through it: naming it, making a conscious choice to act on the anger, learning from the experience so that it will not be repeated, and then letting it go.

The last step, letting go of the anger, is important. The anger that sits within us keeps us from growing.

I have seen many women who were angry enough to end a destructive relationship but never let it go. Just mention the name of the individual 10 years later and watch the anger fester. This is the anger that keeps us stuck and prevents personal growth.

If you find yourself stuck in old anger, ask yourself what benefit you are deriving from holding onto that anger. You may find that looking at it from this angle frees you. In our victim-bound society, being a victim may give you status with some people. Remaining in a victim role, being able to say, "Look at how injured I was," may have served to keep you from facing other areas of your life that need change. Harboring grudges may have given you a sense of superiority over the person who injured you. But the question will always remain, "Now what am I going to do about it?"

Looking at the situation from the perspective of the unity of all life can be freeing. I look back over my life and wish for more incidences of love and affirmation from my father. How I struggled to win his approval. He valued education, so I studied hard and brought home excellent grades. He valued accomplishment, so I worked my way up to first chair in the junior high orchestra, news editor of the school paper, and starting center of the field hockey team—overachiever personified. By high school I had given up, dropping out of most of my activities. Why bother? I had not yet learned to pursue activities for their own sake. I thought that I needed outside approval and praise, which never seemed forthcoming.

It took years before I began to understand that my father could never give me what I was looking for. I thought about the German macho culture in which he was raised. I thought about how he never wanted conceited children. To accomplish this, he consciously withheld praise.

Finally, at his funeral, people that I scarcely knew came up to me and told me how proud my father was of me. He had regaled them with tales of my accomplishments—all unbeknownst to me.

Old anger had festered for years. Finally, I used this anger at him for the emotional damage in my life as the catalyst to learn new ways of relating to other people. I learned a great deal about myself and others in the process, a process that took years of hurting and learning and letting go. It was not easy, but now I can remember my father with affection rather than anger. I can appreciate the good he gave me—a sense of discipline, strong work values, and integrity.

From all this I also learned that you cannot get out of others what they cannot give. I have stopped having unrealistic expectations of others in my life.

By realizing the underlying connectedness in all people, you can transcend anger and begin letting it go even as it develops. When you connect with the divine in the other, you see that person with compassion, realizing that they are injuring themselves with their actions. You can still choose to move out of the way of an individual, but you do not take any anger with you in the move. You move out of love for yourself and the other.

Greed, The Bottomless Bucket

From our insecurity arises the impulse to get and have whatever will bolster our egos. It may be money, clothes, cars, power, prestige, praise, children, houses, antiques. But greed never does what you hope it will. It can never fill the emptiness of the psyche.

Greed can also be described as lust or desire in this sense. The classic story of Howard Hughes as a man who accumulated unparalleled wealth but died an unhappy man leaps to the front of the mind. Smaller addictions often go unnoticed. Some people try to fill their empty space with food, others with sex. The drive for power pushes people to lie and step on fellow employees in a futile climb upward. Even the top position will not satisfy. You are pouring water into a bucket with a giant hole in the bottom.

Jesus taught his disciples, "Sell your possessions and give alms. Make purses for yourselves that do not wear out, an unfailing treasure in heaven, where no thief comes near and no moth destroys" (Luke 12:33).

Once again, the great teachers of wisdom are concerned for our well-being. Just as fear and anger destroy, greed can eat away at our souls. Generosity is valued not only for the help that it gives to the poor but also for the understanding that it teaches the giver. Lust, gluttony, and covetousness all make the list of the seven deadly sins. They are all related to greed. (Note that the other four—pride, anger, envy, and sloth—are also related to poor self-esteem.)

Our wants keep us unhappy. When standing in the dressing room of Macy's, we believe that the beautiful dress that we have tried on will transform us before others. What we forget is that an entire closetful of clothes sits unworn because those dresses could not fulfill the same dream that we have for this new one.

Of course, we periodically need a new outfit. But why? Because our job demands that we look professional or because we appreciate its workmanship and will appreciate it for a long time? Or is it because we think that the clothes have some inherent esteem enhancer sewn into the seams? We require basic necessities in life of housing, food, and clothing. But when is enough enough?

Greed erodes our sense of ethics and morals. We forget what is important and rationalize unnecessary acquisitions. On a local level, we watch relatives fight over an inheritance. On a national level, we watch one retail chain drive another out of business. On a global level, nations murder for the sake of power and land acquisition. When I took an informal survey of my friends concerning greed, the general response I received was, "Greed is at the bottom of all our problems."

Greed and desire cannot merely be repressed. They must be uprooted through a driving wish to be satisfied with need fulfillment, not "want" fulfillment. Recognition of this emotion is necessary. A peaceful and heightened sense of self, realized through meditation, is the most important step that you can make toward ridding yourself of this problem. Then begin to identify where your weaknesses lie.

When John and I built our new home, we had only one small storage closet installed. No longer would we accumulate stuff. Many of our possessions are not only useful but also quite nice.

We decided, however, that when we no longer needed them we would give them away. Cartons of old books that used to sit on bookshelves untouched after initial readings were donated to the local library. Old clothes were given to missions. Our motto is, "If we haven't used it in two years, out it goes." We possess our belongings. They do not possess us.

These actions have freed us from becoming attached to possessions. We know that they will pass from us all too soon. We garner nothing from them except their current usefulness. We also hope that we have saved our children from the burdensome task of disposing of our belongings in later years. We are learning to distinguish between needs and wants. Nothing—no riches, no person—can fill the void in an empty soul. "For where your treasure is, there your heart will be also" (Luke 12:34).

Living free of fear, anger, and greed builds self-esteem. You have chosen to rule your emotions; they do not rule you. You can be cautious when reason tells you to be cautious, but you will not have reflexive fear in inappropriate situations. You can respond to negative actions against you with emotion that moves you to act, but you will not seethe with destructive anger. You can buy items for living, but your purchases will be based on need and not compulsion. The realization that acting on emotions are a choice that you make gives you control over them. You will feel better about yourself, and you will live in greater harmony with all other creatures.

Exercises: Finding Unity

1. List four things that you fear. Select one of them and make a detailed plan to combat that fear. (Examples: climb a ladder with someone's help; apply for a new job; take someone with you as you drive at night; speak up at a meeting.) Now do it. I recommend Susan Jeffers's book, *Feel the Fear and Do It Anyway*, to help with this process.

2. If you have a dragon (some fear that overwhelms you) in your life, try this meditation. Sit in a quiet room with your eyes closed. Picture your fear. Now, move toward it as the little girl in the dragon story did. Keep moving. Picture the object of your fear getting smaller as you approach it. Pick it up in your hand. See how small it really is. Put it back down. Slowly, open your eyes and think about how you feel.

3. Name someone toward whom you feel anger. Answer the following:

   « What precipitated the anger?

   « How long have you felt this way?

   « What possibility exists for reconciliation? If this
    is possible, plan to contact the individual for

conversation. If this would be harmful to you, write out the imaginary dialogue.

‹ What personal changes—both positive and negative—have come about from this anger?

‹ What do you know about this person that would explain his or her behavior?

If this anger is still destructive to you at this point, try releasing it. This will probably take many tries, but should become easier each time.

Sit in a meditative state. Picture the other person. Now, picture a white light moving from you to that person and encompassing both of you. Repeat this several times until the response feels natural.

Decide how you will take what you have learned from this encounter and use it positively in other relationships.

If you remain stuck in your anger, seek professional help.

4. Clean out a closet. Donate items that you no longer wear to a local charity.

5. What are your treasures? What do they tell you about your heart?

7

Outside the Self

"How wonderful it is that nobody
need wait a single moment before starting
to improve the world."

—Anne Frank, *DIARY OF A YOUNG GIRL*[1]

Living with Integrity

Growing up in suburban America in the 1950s, for all of its drawbacks, was simple. Life was structured. I went to school, practiced the piano every day for 30 minutes, attended Girl Scouts on Tuesday afternoon, and went to Sunday school and church each Sunday morning. The theme of life was, "do good and good will come to you."

I memorized not only the motto and slogan from Scouts, "Be prepared" and "Do a good turn daily," but also the 10 Girl Scout Laws beginning with "A Girl Scout's honor is to be trusted." I learned the Ten Commandments in Sunday school. On camping trips I learned to leave a place cleaner than I found it and to "take only pictures, leave only footprints."

In sheltered middle-class America, I assumed that everyone else lived as I had been taught. Part of the rude awakening of adulthood was the realization that many people are not honorable. To manipulate you, they will tell you what you want to hear. While I had promised to "help other people at all times," another code existed that said, "I will do whatever it takes to get ahead," or as one boy learned from another scout at camp, "On my honor I will do my best to help myself and cheat the rest."

Re-evaluating ethics to live in an adult world was part of growing up and becoming independent. When people long for the "good old days," I believe they are wishing for the times when they still believed that everyone operated out of altruism and not self-centeredness.

To abandon values that other people call naive may be more detrimental to self-esteem than might initially be assumed. After all, wouldn't getting ahead in life be esteem-enhancing?

During the 1960s, Colin Fletcher wrote *Situation Ethics*. His purpose was to show that not all values are strictly black and white. Should we be completely honest when honesty will harm the other person? Is it acceptable to belong to a racially exclusive organization if that organization provides important service for others? Shades of gray appeared more acceptable than I had been taught.

Over the last 30 years some colleges have been forced to abandon ethical codes of honor for exams. In the late 1980s, my son ran a high school project on cheating. Ben passed out confidential surveys in each homeroom class and found that over 80 percent of the students in his high school had cheated during that school year. His informal study showed that passing was more important than personal integrity. What, however, was happening to self-esteem in the process?

How you conduct your life has profound impact on how you view yourself. It may seem unfair that Newt Gingrich asked his wife for a divorce when she was lying in the hospital with cancer but went on to become Speaker of the House anyway. Ethics may seem a thing of the past when Dick Morris, former adviser to President Bill Clinton, cheats on his wife with a prostitute and produces a love child with another woman and then earns $2.5 million to write a book about what a genius he is. Why bother to be good when the plumber constantly over-charges people, lies to them about their plumbing problems, but lives in a beautiful house on the Long Island Sound?

Why bother to be honest, if you, too, can cheat on your exams, pay less taxes than you should, or have an ego-pleasing fling on the side without anyone knowing?

Why bother? Because your internal register will chalk up the cost. You may receive temporary gratification from unethical actions unbeknownst to anyone else, but your insides know the difference.

The success of 12-step addictions programs based on Alcoholics Anonymous depends on individual accountability for past actions. Giving up drinking is not enough. The recovering individual makes amends to those he or she has harmed because of addiction. Then the alcoholic can move forward in sobriety. Living honorably is as important in recovery as switching from beer to soda.

Universal Codes of Behavior

All religions have codes of conduct, which serve two major purposes. The first is to help a group live together in community. When the Hebrews left Egypt as a scraggly tribe wandering across the desert, the Ten Commandments provided a framework for living together. Later, volumes of other rules in Leviticus and Deuteronomy evolved within that theocracy as legal systems.

The second purpose for a code of conduct is to help an individual achieve a spiritual ideal. One example is the Eightfold Path of Buddhism, which delineates the way for an individual to overcome delusions about life and achieve nirvana.

The resurgent Goddess movement, which avoids lists of rules because rules are often confining for women, still has one universal adage: "Do no harm."

The Tao Te Ching, the fundamental text of Taoism, is the most translated book in the world next to the Bible and the Bhagavad Gita. It is the centerpiece of Chinese religion and thought. *Tao* means "the way" and prescribes a way of living that can unite the follower with the way of ultimate reality.

This classic scripture tells us to treat everyone well, both those who are good and those who are not good. In so doing, we achieve goodness.

It tells us that when we are compassionate and frugal we will be brave and magnanimous. It is when we do not try to get ahead of others that we become worthy leaders.

According to the Tao, simplicity, patience, and compassion are three important virtues. To possess these brings great treasures. To chase after money and security closes your heart. To worry about others' approval makes you their prisoner.

Peace is also a high value. Weapons are instruments of fear, and decent people avoid them except in the most extreme necessity.

The Tao, like Jesus, teaches that to obtain everything, you must give everything up.

As with other scriptures, the Tao advocates a path that is not based on striving for success. "The bright Way seems dim. The forward Way seems backward."[2] It is a path based on integrity.

Buddhism advocates an Eightfold Path. This path includes:

1. Right views, beliefs concerning what being a human means

2. Right intent, a desire to move our lives toward enlightenment and right living

3. Right speech, to speak truthfully to all and charitably about others

4. Right conduct, which involves specific precepts for living

5. Right livelihood, working in occupations that promote life rather than destroy it

6. Right effort, the realization that self-discipline and a strong will are necessary to put right living into practice

7. Right mindfulness, realizing that we are what we think and that we can change ourselves by changing how we think

8. Right concentration, which involves the practice of meditation

The list of precepts for the fourth step of the Eightfold Path, right conduct, is not unlike the second half of the Ten Commandments: Do not kill, which includes animals (strict Buddhists are vegetarians). Do not steal.

SELF AND SOUL

Do not lie. Do not be unchaste. Do not drink intoxicants.

The Ten Commandments, after the first four which define a relationship with the Hebrew God, also prescribe tenets for living: Honor your father and your mother. You shall not kill. You shall not commit adultery. You shall not steal. You shall not bear false witness. You shall not covet.

Perhaps the easiest of all virtues to remember from religions is the Golden Rule, expressed in some form in all faiths, "Do unto others as you would have them do unto you." It is easily recognized in the words of Jesus, "Love your neighbor as yourself."

When we adhere to principles of living, we live with integrity. Our actions reflect our words. When that happens, others will trust us and we will trust and respect ourselves.

Conversely, when we violate these standards, we diminish both our sense of ourselves and the well-being of our souls. Remember that lying, cheating, and other forms of dishonesty are symptoms of addiction and that addiction is both a spiritual and physical disease. To be emotionally healthy with high self-esteem, practice a life of integrity.

Helen's former boss owed her $182 in reimbursable expenses, but no matter how many times she approached her, Helen was put off. Talk of embezzlement circulated around the company. Suspicions about this employer accelerated. Helen's minister father summed up the situation succinctly when he exclaimed, "Why, Helen, you must tell your boss to pay you. Her soul is in jeopardy."

Claiming Ownership

When we are young, we learn our standards of behavior from others, often from leaders of our faith and from our family. Part of maturing is sorting through these values and deciding which hold true for us and which may not.

In chapter 2 it is noted that, over time, culture absorbed and defined religion. Additional lists of "shoulds" appeared that affected women. While the early Christian community had women as bishops and priests, by the third century it was a male-only ruling class. Although their precepts advocate equality, both Confucianism and Buddhism have emerged in the same way. Mohammed believed in the equality of the sexes. Today, Islam has women behind veils. Supremacy of men, subordination in marriage, and nonuse or limited use of birth control are examples of tenets given to women through religion that may be re-evaluated and even given up completely while more universal values are claimed and owned.

Before Pope John Paul's visit to the United States in October 1995, a telephone poll was taken of U.S. Roman Catholics. Eighty percent of them felt that it is possible to disagree with the Pope on official positions on morality and still be a good Catholic. Issues cited include birth control and abortion, both condemned by the Roman Catholic Church.[3] This did not necessarily mean that 80 percent of Catholics use birth control regularly—in fact, 59 percent said that they had. Instead, it showed decisions based on personal values and the acceptance of other people having the right to make similar decisions for themselves.

Deciding which values to uphold and then living by them is an essential part of maturity and self-regard. When values become ours rather than ones merely handed down by others, they become an integral part of our lives. We live what we say we believe, or as recovering addicts often claim, we "walk our talk." The more we live with integrity, the more we expect it of ourselves and the more we "value our values."

A choice to operate out of high ethical values goes beyond your own life. My decision not to eat meat is not only good for my body (and the animals I'm not eating), but also good for the planet. Less land and water are needed to grow vegetables than to raise cattle. That means more food for more people and less destruction of plains and prairies through overgrazing. Rain forests in South America do not have to be razed in order to create more pasture land for beef herding. My family benefits because I have more energy to care for them. Everyone wins.

If everyone filled out their tax forms honestly, our country would be richer; in fact, fewer taxes would need to be levied to compensate for lost revenue through cheating and the hiring of IRS agents. You win as a taxpayer through self-validation of an ethical system, and all taxpayers win through lower taxes.

Outside the Self

Selfless Service

Beth came storming into my church office one Monday morning. "How could you preach what you did yesterday?" she asked as she plopped into the chair across from my desk. "After three months of telling me that I have to set boundaries and claim myself, you stand in the pulpit and talk about denying yourself. I was so angry and confused that I didn't sleep at all last night."

Self-denial, self-sacrifice, selfless service. These principal phrases are taught in all major religions as a way to achieve eternal peace. Yet these same lessons have been used as weapons of subordination by those in positions of dominance. How could yesterday's sermon make sense to Beth?

Beth had come up against the hardest precept of faith to reconcile with emerging as a woman of self-worth—the concept of self-denial. We had spent many weeks together in counseling sessions trying to unpack an upbringing that had taught her that a woman must be self-sacrificing for others. She had worked hard to begin training her children to pick up after themselves instead of doing it for them. She had started to claim boundaries when her friend called at inconvenient times. It had been a struggle for Beth to learn to say, "This is not a good time. Can I call you back?" without feeling guilty that she was letting down a friend. It had required a joint session with her husband, Dave, to begin new habits of cooperation with home tasks. Beth learned that Dave was more than willing to help, but he needed direction to unlearn being waited on constantly. It had taken a physical and emotional collapse to bring Beth to the point of seeking help. She felt guilty when she was not serving others. It was the biggest obstacle to her progress.

Now, she thought that her pastor/counselor had given contradictory advice from the pulpit. I lost my integrity in her eyes because of the seeming inconsistency.

The biblical text for the previous day's sermon was Jesus' teachings on discipleship found in Mark 8 (also in Matthew 16 and Luke 9): "If any want to become my followers, let them deny themselves and take up their cross and follow me. For those who want to save their life will lose it, and those who lose their life for my sake, and for the sake of the gospel, will save it" (Mark 8:24–35).

I pulled out the manuscript of my sermon, and we reread parts of it together. "We are called to deny ourselves and take up our crosses. I need to caution one thing. Self-denial is not pulling oneself down and allowing others to put us down. As strongly as I believe that denying self is essential to the gospel, I often see those who equate this with having low self-esteem. You are a child of God, and as a disciple of Jesus, you are worthy. Denying self means, instead, to place our lives, our values, and our priorities under the power of the gospel. We allow the gospel—not others, not ourselves—to be the shaper and corrector and transformer of who we are.

OUTSIDE THE SELF

"You see, crosses are ones that we pick up intentionally. They are not situations in our lives imposed from elsewhere. They are not illnesses, nasty employers, or disrespectful children. You know that slaves were told that their slavery was a cross to carry, that God would bless them for it. It was not. It was slavery, a wrong that needed to be corrected. Crosses are voluntarily carried by each individual in life. The only valid crosses in life are ones that we, of our own free choice, bear."

Beth paused. "Okay. When I thought that I had no choice but to let everyone walk over me, that wasn't a cross."

"Right," I confirmed.

"But if I really want to help with a cause, because I feel strongly about it, that could be 'good' self-denial."

"Right again," I replied.

We finished the joint reading of the sermon: "I cannot tell you what your cross looks like. There will be times in your life when you will say 'yes' or 'no' to some request or some need or some inner urging. You will need to decide for yourself."

Beth realized that just hearing the scripture had triggered her old messages about service. We looked at her life once more in terms of this religious adage.

Beth understood that being a doormat for others was helpful to neither herself nor them. In order to teach self-sufficiency to her children, she needed them to be responsible for their belongings. In order to enhance a caring relationship, Dave needed opportunity to do some of the caregiving. What could Beth do that was selfless service?

To deny oneself means to give up being self-centered. It also requires having a solid sense of self to set aside. Beth began to spend one hour a week volunteering at the community hospital. She was given the simple task of delivering flowers to patients' rooms.

What amazed her was how quickly she began to care about the well-being of total strangers and how much her smiling presence meant to others. This was service that she freely chose, not obligation placed on her by family or through her own guilt. She understands the difference.

Living beyond the Self

A major criticism of current America is its self-centeredness. Even volunteerism can become a calculation of benefits for the giver instead of the receiver. In fact, many westerners have embraced Eastern religions because they can escape into themselves through meditation rather than use meditation as a vehicle for changing themselves into other-centered people.

Victor Sogen Hori, a Japanese-Canadian religion professor, argues that American Buddhists have imposed Western notions of autonomy and individualism on Buddhism and have imported only those parts of the religion that affirm American values. He cites as an example a week's retreat. The Anglo-Americans who attended said that the meditations were useful for self-understanding and self-realization. The Chinese-Americans who attended said that the meditations were an opportunity to reflect on their shortcomings in dealing with others.[4] Same meditations, different perspectives.

Doing for others with no expectation of personal gain is key to well-being and spiritual development. It enhances our sense of connectedness with all creation, one of the seven universal principles of faith. We realize that we are the people that we help, just as we are the people who help us. When my neighbor, the new mother of a two-month-old, was ill, I cared for her baby and three-year-old for four days while she recovered. "How can I repay you?" she asked. "Do the same for someone else someday" was the only appropriate response that I could think of.

Many women are able to achieve service within their families. They are the ones who find contentment in homemaking as a career. But for women for whom homemaking is a financial trade-off for security or a family expectation or whose interests and talents lie elsewhere, inner satisfaction is often lacking. They might need a career or volunteer responsibilities beyond the home for personal satisfaction.

Our spirituality and self-esteem begin within ourselves but continue to grow when lived out in relationship to others.

I agree with Natalia Ginzburg, who said in *The Little Virtues*, "As far as the education of children is concerned I think they should be taught not the little virtues but the great ones. Not thrift but generosity and an indifference to money; not caution but courage and a contempt for danger; not shrewdness but frankness and a love of truth; not tact but love for one's neighbor and self-denial; not desire for success but a desire to be and to know."[5]

Exercises: Living with Integrity

1. Make a list of the principles for living that you learned as a child from your parents, your faith, and other organizations to which you belonged. Mark which ones you still consider valid and helpful. Which ones do you find constricting? Why?

2. From the above list, take personal inventory. Do your daily actions match your beliefs? Do you need to make changes to bring your living in line with your believing? Begin to make these changes and notice how you feel.

3. Do you find that you are forced to live by values that you do not respect, such as covering up at work or lying or keeping secrets at home? What would happen if you refused to live by these values? Find a friend and discuss.

4. What service do you give? If none, plan one act of giving for someone else this week.

8

The Virtues of Faith

*"My dear, we must need another
lesson in patience."*

—the author to her husband at a
congested traffic intersection

Gifts or Self-Will?

In Paul's letter to the Galatians, the apostle
names nine virtues that became hallmarks for
people of the Christian faith: love, joy, peace,
patience, kindness, generosity, faithfulness, gentleness, and self-control (Galatians 5:22). When taken
out of their biblical context, these personality
characteristics are often listed as feminine virtues.
"There they go again," the chant begins. "Forcing

women into meek and mild roles, just when we began learning to assert ourselves and take control of our lives. They're trying to push us back down."

Interestingly enough, however, Paul was addressing a primarily male audience in his letter to the Galatian church and was holding up what we call traditionally feminine values as ideals for everyone.[1] He stated that those who are "in the spirit"—that is, spiritually centered—will exhibit these traits. They are also traits demonstrated by one who has established self-esteem.

"You know, there is a certain amount of truth to that," Sharon volunteered at a weekend retreat. "Since I feel better about myself, I listen more to my inner wisdom, and I don't need to be as aggressive with others. I can be more kind and generous because I know that I won't let others walk over me. I can be kinder in a firm way and generous without being taken from. There is a difference.

"Yes, once I was afraid of these virtues—if that's what you want to call them—because I thought they meant weakness. Now I see that I operate from strength when I embody them.

"But—" Sharon continued, "and this is an important but—the self-esteem had to come first. If I just tried to be nice for nice's sake, people instinctively knew where my weaknesses were and could zero right in on them."

Sharon hit an important key that is very much an element of Paul's writing: The goodness or excellence that comes from within arises from strength. It is not imposed from without as a "should" or "ought" but seeps throughout our being like spilled ink permeates a piece of cloth.

Paul calls them fruits of the Spirit—evidences, in the way that we live our lives, that we have found our spiritual selves.

What about these fruits? Are they virtues that we can cultivate, or are they "gifts" that come to us from within? Do we teach ourselves patience, or are we endowed with it from an inner source? Can we successfully control ourselves, or does self-control come naturally to those who have mastered some higher truth? Are some people gentle by nature and others brusque, or can we impose gentleness as a standard and live more tenderly with others?

Buddhism tells us to cultivate four qualities that are considered divine conditions of the mind: compassion, loving-kindness, sympathetic joy, and equanimity. Do we need a divine mind in order to cultivate them, or by cultivating them does our mind become closer to the divine? Which comes first, the chicken or the egg?

I believe that the answer is both. Let us look at four virtues extolled by all faiths: patience, gentleness, self-control, and forgiveness.

Patience

Patience seems like such a trivial virtue. So what if I mutter at the slow driver of the car in front of me at a four-way stop? So what if I hustle my child's cleanup by picking up half her toys for her? So what if I walk faster than my grandmother as we walk through the mall? So what if I want my employee's report before its due date? Do these things really make a difference?

What is patience? J. I. Rodale's *The Synonym Finder* offers other words that highlight the importance of this human characteristic: composure, containment, poise, self-possession, serenity, even-temperedness, forbearance, endurance, sufferance, stamina, indefatigability, perseverance, constancy, and many more.[2]

When we are impatient with others, it is because we judge them. They are not as fast or competent or quick-minded as we think they ought to be. But look closer at the reflection that our judgments cast upon us.

I confess that I did not enjoy my children's early childhood years. All Doug ever wanted to do (or so it seemed) was play Candy Land. I hated Candy Land. So I sat on the floor, thinking of all the "important" things that I should be doing while my son slowly moved his token across the board. I let him win, thinking that it would satisfy him and that I could get on with my life. Never. His interest went from Candy Land to other more time-consuming and complicated board games. Hooray, I thought, when he outgrew that stage.

What, I now wonder, could have been more important than those hours on the floor with Doug? The laundry? Fixing dinner? The nonprofit board of which I was president? My impatience said far more about me than it ever did about my three-year-old. I simply thought that my agenda was more significant than his. So it is with patience.

A common misconception is that patience is an inborn quality and that nothing we can do will alter it. In fact, patience can be learned. I began to make a game of it. Lessons in Patience, I dubbed my experiment.

And so, at the congested intersection when we had not planned our time well and we thought others were responsible for our lateness, I learned to say, "My dear, we must need another lesson in patience." My husband still shoots dirty looks when I issue this utterance, but he understands my point. Patience is an internal condition. We can make a daily conscious decision to alter the condition of impatience. When something holds me up, I see yet again that I have not learned all that I need to about patience. This new attitude allows me to sit back and relax. It is time for me to learn, not for someone else to hurry faster.

Patience does not mean seething inside while waiting for something to happen. It means letting life take its course in its own time. Letting Doug grow and learn at his own pace. Letting Grandma set the pace at the mall. Allowing employees to turn reports in as scheduled. Moving forward when the traffic allows.

THE VIRTUES OF FAITH

Patience also has a great deal to do with self-esteem—feeling comfortable enough to be patient with our own lives.

"I wanted to be perfect, beyond reproach," confided Louise. "But my insecurity led me to over-train, until finally I injured myself and had to rest. It was only after the crisis that I learned to be patient with myself."

Louise was a high school basketball star who won a full scholarship to college. Used to being the best on her team, her ego plummeted when she arrived for training in August before her freshman year. Her layups were easily deflected by the defense. Other young women quickly outran her on the court. A panic set in. What if she sat on the bench all year? Could she stand the loss of the accolades that she was accustomed to? Her coach assured her that her skills would improve to meet the new challenges, and she gave Louise special exercises to develop her weak spots.

Impatient to become number one again, Louise overexercised, until the inevitable happened. She found herself icing a badly sprained ankle while she watched the rest of the team play.

"My sense of self had become so completely entangled with my ability to play basketball that I lost all perspective. The forced rest gave me time to see the tension that I had created within myself. I had to learn to build my skills and strength slowly and patiently or face never playing college basketball again. Fortunately, I had a great coach. Not only could she convey technical skills in manipulating a ball but also she was superb at understanding a young woman's ego needs. She taught me to like myself enough to let my body heal and build slowly. She taught me patience."

There is, in all these virtues, what I call a crossover point—the point where we stop seething inside, repeating to ourselves, "I will be patient, I will be patient" and we simply are patient. We don't think about it. We naturally say to the person in front of us at the checkout counter, "Take your time. It's fine," without even thinking about all the other reasons we could have for wanting to pay for our things more quickly. We achieve a new level of consciousness, a new inner peace that precludes the turmoil and agitation that previously fed our impatience. It just isn't there.

If meditation helps calm the mind, then patience is indeed a fruit of the spirit. It is carrying the stillness of the mind we gained in our early-morning hours with us all day. It is an important skill.

Gentleness

In previous generations, the highest compliment one could receive was to be called a gentlewoman or gentleman. While that statement often connoted a certain level of high breeding, it always assumed certain qualities:

generosity, kindness, compassion, warmth, graciousness, thoughtfulness, mercy, tenderheartedness. Today, gentleness is equated with weakness—the antithesis of "successful" behavior.

It is this image of spirituality as weakness that has kept men away from a religious life. In the United States, women have historically far outnumbered men in Christian church attendance. During various eras of revivals, the "soldier of Christ" was used as a metaphor to attract men to the faith. Warriors going off to conquer the world for good and fend off evil marched bravely out of the sanctuary Sunday morning. Evangelist Billy Sunday used this technique to bring absentee men back to the fold. "Lord, save us from offhanded, flabby-cheeked, brittle-boned, weak-kneed, thin-skinned, pliable, plastic, spineless, effeminate, sissified, three-carat Christianity," he pleaded from the pulpit.[3] A man could be "manly" and still have faith. Church attendance rose.

Psychotherapist Anne Wilson Schaef, Ph.D., in her seminal book, *Women's Reality*,[4] addresses this point. She says that reality has been defined by the patriarchal system for years. Reality for most people is a world of power: One has power over another; one is powerless in front of another. There is another, quite viable system of reality—one of equality and partnership.

We can be gentle with one another. Our reality does not have to be that of the warrior carrying weapons. Our internal strength allows us to operate without coercion. Gentleness is not a weakness but a strength.

When we have experienced the unity of all life and understand that we are connected to all others, we realize that lack of gentleness or compassion for another is lack of gentleness or compassion for ourselves. The scriptures are true: As we do to another we do to ourselves. We can be gentle with another because we respect ourselves enough to know that we do not want to be brutish with anyone or anything. Children and dogs can learn best without hitting and belittling. They respond to gentleness. They understand caring. All creatures do.

Self-esteem and spirituality play upon each other once again. Gentleness comes from a strong self. Being gentle is a beginning for developing a sense of self. You like yourself better when you strive to be compassionate and understanding with others. When you judge and criticize, you will subconsciously feel criticism for yourself, even if you do not acknowledge it on a conscious level.

It is amazing how little is written on the virtue of gentleness. We are afraid of the concept. As women we have struggled inordinately to dismantle the old shackles of how we ought to behave. We don't want to be taken advantage of; we don't want to be abused.

Gentleness and strength are not opposites: They are complementary. When you are no longer afraid of gentleness, you have altered your reality. Your reality now says that there is more than one way to view life and that you will no longer view it from a competitive, hierarchical vantage point. You are well on your way to a reality that honors a spiritually integrated self.

Self-Control

"Telling me to control my urge for sweets is like telling me to gain 10 pounds. The more I try to control myself, the more I eat." So the lament goes in some form or another for thousands of women today. "My intentions are good. I just can't control myself."

If there is any virtue that I would label a gift of grace, it would be that of self-control. To try to impose discipline on oneself is like trying to hold an inflated ball under water. Just when we think we have it under control, it pops up somewhere else.

Self-control has been confused with law and order: Thou shalt not. Yet a rigid person is not a self-disciplined person. An unyielding manner, in fact, is a sure sign that all is not well within, that a struggle is occurring, and that we are determined to master some undesired craving.

Eastern religions teach us to "train the senses." This is not meant as a rigid discipline but as a discipline in conjunction with bringing the personal self into a unitive state with the eternal self. Richard Foster, in his *Study Guide for Celebration of Discipline*, puts it this way: "In time, we found that solitude did not give us power to win the rat race; on the contrary, it taught us to ignore the struggle altogether."[5]

What Foster is saying applies to self-control. There comes a point in your spiritual journey when you no longer obsess or think about that which needs to be controlled. Chocolate, alcohol, money, and power no longer need to be controlled. Because your spirit leads you, your ego-centered agenda does not. It cannot dictate your wants. When it tries, your inner self is strong enough to brush the idea away quickly. Meditation is one of the best first steps in dieting.

Self-control is an antidote to the "me-ism" of modern American society. It is a virtue of faith because of the inner strength that it calls forth. Twelve-step programs know that an inner spiritual life is essential to mastery over addictions: The first step is to admit that you (your ego, that is) cannot accomplish the task on your own. You (your spiritual self), however, can.

All compulsions stem from a weak self. That is why strong self-esteem is so important to obtaining release and why self-esteem based on an inner spiritual strength is a must.

Corrine began meditating four years ago. She enjoyed the peacefulness that it brought to her day, and she was less perturbed at others. She liked herself more. "It was gradual. I'd be cautious to say that all of my growth came just from meditating. I was doing a lot of other reading and working on issues from several fronts at once. But I certainly felt stronger as the changes occurred. It became circular—the stronger I got, the deeper my meditation became and the deeper my meditation, the better I felt about myself.

"Over time I noticed that things that I compulsed about were less important. I had tried a thousand times, just like everyone else has, to quit smoking. When I finally decided to quit three years ago, it was amazingly easy. Not that I didn't have bad days, mind you. It wasn't perfect. It's just that long periods of time went by when I didn't even think about a cigarette. Before, trying to quit meant constantly having thoughts of cigarettes flash before my eyes. I tried repeating a mantra when a craving started this time, and it helped. Meditation made a difference."

To look at Corrine today, one could not tell that she used to have a problem with either tobacco or food. "I thought less about my other 'fixes' also," she continued. "A week could go by without my wanting ice cream, then two. I find now that about the only time I still really have cravings is when I'm super-stressed at work. But I've learned that the important thing is to look at the stress. When I don't let it get away from me, I am able to use my meditation to control my anxiety until the pressure lets up. It helps me subdue my anger at the incompetence at work, too.

"By the way," Corrine adds, "I can enjoy a dish of ice

cream now without wanting to eat the entire half-gallon. I used to think that I shouldn't have any at all. Now it is just another food to enjoy occasionally."

Typically, Corrine notices her friends dismissing her new freedom from addiction to tobacco and food as, "You're different from me. You don't understand. You have self-control." She doesn't even try to explain. She knows that they must travel their own journey in their own time.

Forgiveness

The issue of forgiveness is steeped in the muck and mire of misinterpretation. Forgiveness is not:

- Letting people off the hook
- Forgetting
- Pretending something never happened
- Pretending that you do not hurt or suffer
- Pretending that the relationship is just like it always was
- Repressing a past deed
- Excusing past actions because of extenuating circumstances

Forgiveness is none of the above.

Forgiveness is a process of healing that takes place when a person gives up resentment which accompanies a past hurt inflicted by another person. Because resentment has been eating at the person who was wronged, forgiveness, in its proper time and place, becomes a gift of emotional health to the wronged person. It never means that the wrongdoer was not at fault.

Amanda's life was filled with abuse for years. Her parents had been strict disciplinarians who believed that "to spare the rod was to spoil the child." Harsh physical and emotional turmoil marked her childhood years. To escape, she married early—into another abusive home life. This time it was her husband, Vincent, who threw vitriolic criticism at her and hit her when "she wouldn't listen."

Through the help of her local domestic violence shelter she finally escaped living the victim's life. She secured employment at a local department store where she also learned to dress fashionably and feel valued. She made enormous strides. Finally, after five years of living on her own, she decided to let go of her past. The only way she knew how was to forgive both her parents and her husband.

Amanda went through several stages to arrive at this point.

1. She named the wrongs that had been done to her. Amanda knew that she could not gloss over any of the details. To do so would mitigate the story.

2. She had to confront the wrong. With her husband, this had been accomplished in court during her divorce proceeding. But because her mother had died of cancer and she'd lost contact with her father, she needed the help of a counselor to confront the rage at her parents.

3. She looked for redress for her hurt. Amanda wished that the courts had awarded her more money. However, there were no children from the marriage, and her state did not recognize alimony once she was employed.

She knew that she deserved better than she received but accepted what she could get. She never did receive an apology from her ex-husband.

4. She moved on with her life. Amanda's financial and emotional independence helped in this step.

5. She began to forgive.

Amanda made a conscious choice to begin the process of forgiveness. Many well-meaning friends had suggested it in the past, but she had not been ready. For years her anger served her, giving her fuel to move forward as a single woman, to "show them all that I am not the miserable person they said."

Five years later Amanda's anger no longer served her well. It was holding her back. Often she festered for hours at a time about her upbringing and marriage, reciting in detail over and over in her mind all that had befallen her. Finally, she realized that the hours she spent rehashing could be better utilized living. She wanted to be a positive person.

"I found," Amanda shared later, "that just the decision to want to forgive was a turning point. It was hard because no one ever asked for my forgiveness. I had to let go of the past as best I could.

"I found myself wavering back and forth. I would spend a few days not even thinking about my parents or Vincent. That was like blue sky peeking through constant clouds. Then the resentment would return, maybe even for a week at a time. Then more blue sky. Then clouds. One day I realized that I was wishing Vincent well, that I hoped his job was going better for him. I surprised myself. That's what forgiveness ended up being for me—being able to wish Vincent well. And I felt better about myself for having reached this point."

Her story is classic. Forgiveness does not come in one fell swoop. We grant it. We take it back. We let go again. One day we realize that it hasn't plagued us for quite a long time. We are able to wish the other person well. We are freed.

Amanda has not whitewashed the issue of abuse by releasing her past. She volunteers now in the same local shelter that helped her to her feet five years ago. She is an effective volunteer because she is able to walk with the victims who come to her for aid without being embroiled in their stories. Her memory reminds her of the importance of her work. She also lobbies politically for change in a system that still allows domestic violence to occur. Her passion now goes to make the world better for others, not to harbor anger and resentment about her past.

"I'm glad that I got to this point." Amanda spoke with confidence behind the women's clothing counter. "I think that my anger and resentments were making me ill. My stomach is much calmer since I was able to forgive. But don't let anyone tell you otherwise—it was hard work. And don't think that now that I am dating I will easily trust all men again. Nothing in my life is sugarcoated that easily."

Forgiveness is a loaded issue because it has been abused. Clergy have sent women back to violent partners to "pray harder and forgive," only to be battered more. It has been used as an easy whitewash by those who do not want to deal with the deep pain that victims of rape, sexual abuse, or other crimes feel. For lesser "offenses," forgiveness has doubled for pretending others did not say what they said about you.

Forgiveness is good for the forgiver. Jesus told his followers that they would be forgiven as they forgave, not because it is a "thou shalt" but because it is good for the soul. It includes forgiving ourselves for our own wrongs.

In 1985, Egypt Air Flight number 648 was highjacked to Malta. When their demands for fuel were not met, the hijackers shot one Israeli or American passenger every 15 minutes. Jackie Pflug was selected. She was shot in the back of the head, assumed dead, and pushed from the plane. Her survival alone was a miracle. Even more of a miracle, she was able to function again, although she still suffers from vision impairment and a learning disability.

Pflug thought that she was well, that her past was behind her. However, recurrent headaches, stomach pains, and sleepless nights plagued her. Finally, she realized that in order to be totally healed from the recurrent nightmare of her ordeal, she would have to do what she previously thought was unthinkable—forgive her assailants.

Pflug wrote, "As long as I held on to bitterness and hatred, I wouldn't heal. If I didn't forgive, I'd continue to be angry and bitter for the rest of my life. And the bitterness and resentment would slowly eat me alive. If I held on to hatred, I'd remain a victim of my attackers for the rest of my life. To be a free person I had to forgive.

"The choice was mine."[6]

She still holds Omar Mohammed Ali Rezaq, the surviving hijacker, accountable for his actions and feels that he should not be released from prison early. Yet she forgives him for what he did to her life. Now she is headache-free and sleeps through the night.

The power of forgiveness—an unquestionable gift of the spirit.

Exercises: Harvesting Fruit

1. Pick two of the virtues of faith (love, joy, peace, patience, kindness, generosity, faithfulness, gentleness, and self-control) that you would like to deepen in your life.

❈ Write down how not being steeped in this virtue affects your life negatively and what specific behavior changes you would like to enact.

❈ Spend five minutes each morning meditating on these virtues.

❈ Do an overt act each day involving these virtues. (Do a favor for a friend; let someone in front of you in the checkout line at the grocery store; donate to charity.)

2. What other virtues are important to you? Make a list.

3. Is there someone in your life against whom you hold a grudge?

❈ If you are ready, seriously consider offering that person forgiveness. An excellent resource for this process is *Forgive and Forget: Healing the Hurts We Don't Deserve*, by Lewis Smedes.

❈ Do not chastise yourself if you are not ready for this step. Remember that forgiveness is a process. Perhaps you will want to consider professional counseling.

4. What do you need to forgive in yourself? Talk to a close friend or counselor about these issues. Free your mind of your own foibles.

9

Examples of Grace: Advice from the Mystics

"My soul experienced a peace so sweet, so deep, it would be impossible to express it. For seven years and a half that inner peace has remained my lot, and has not abandoned me in the midst of the greatest trials."

—Saint Therese of Lisieux[1]

❦

Mystical Experience

Mysticism conjures up images of hocus-pocus, of gurus sitting pretzel-fashion in a cloud of burning incense, of psychotic individuals standing on street corners proclaiming some new (or old) "truth." Mysticism is none of these.

Nothing inspires me more than reading and studying stories of mystics—those who have found the voice of their god within themselves and followed that voice. The validation that these women (and men) develop is a testimony to the high level of self-regard that we can possess when our spiritual lives are centered.

The term *mystic* refers to someone who has had a spiritual experience—*experience* being the key word—during which he or she discovers that the ultimate reality or source of all being lives within. The mystic, then, is one who has the unitive experience with the divine referred to throughout this book, especially in chapter 4. As Saint Catherine was quoted there, "My me is God."

Anne Bancroft, writer and teacher of mysticism, outlines three essential tenets of mysticism in her book, *The Luminous Vision*. First, our "beingness" is that of the ultimate or God-center. Second, in order to find this unconditioned beingness, we must let go of our dependence on worldly things. Third, when we do let go, the nature of our true life as a human being is revealed to us.[2] These beliefs are found in all religions. The foundations of universal religions listed in chapter 3 are merely different wordings of Bancroft's essential teachings of mysticism.

Mysticism is not magic. Magic strives to change what exists or to manipulate nature. Mysticism is the discovery of our essential nature and our unity with all others, because everyone possesses the same essential nature.

Bancroft goes on to say that a mystic no longer is bound by feelings of oppression and insecurity that arise when we consider ourselves as separate from the rest of the world. A deep sense of the inner self guides the mystic who knows this sense is the "miraculous God-ground." "The expression of this living is in spontaneous and joyful self-giving."[3]

What a testimony to self-esteem through spiritual centeredness—freedom from feelings of oppression and insecurity. No more victim mentality. No more inferior feelings. But is it doable?

What kind of life might a woman have who grounds herself in spiritual experiences? We will look at three different women from three different eras and three different traditions. Each of them will speak out of her own culture, but the similarities are striking.

Our earlier principles of self-esteem stated that a person of self-worth:

- « Has a sense of reality and lives consciously, not in a fantasy world
- « Is able to alter her reality through goals and purpose
- « Has clear boundaries concerning who she is and is not bound to other people for her self-definition
- « Lives with integrity

Examples of Grace: Advice from the Mystics

We will see how these principles operate within the framework of these women's lives.

Self-esteem, as we describe it, was not an issue to a woman living in the Middle Ages in England or in the sixteenth century in India. People thought in terms of community, not the self. Yet in order to break out of traditional molds, women would have had to have deep inner strength. Julian of Norwich, a contemporary of Chaucer in fourteenth-century England, was the first woman to write a book in English—a book about her spiritual visions. Meera was a sixteenth-century poet-saint of India who dared to abandon her husband—the most radical action a Hindu woman could take—and her life of privilege. They called her mad, yet centuries later she was the symbol that Mahatma Gandhi chose for his independence movement. Peace Pilgrim wandered the roads of the United States, Canada, and Mexico for 28 years from 1953 to 1981, walking over 25,000 miles to promote peace. Different times. Different cultures. Different faith backgrounds. Yet their stories are remarkably the same.

Julian of Norwich

Author Virginia Woolf's admonition that a woman must have a room of her own draws nods of approval from women everywhere. Julian's room, however, is probably more than most would want. She was an anchoress.

Anchorites were known in early Christianity as those who retreated to the desert for undisturbed prayer. An anchoress in the fourteenth century withdrew to a room for life, although this was not as austere as first impressions might indicate. Julian's room was an enclosure built on the side of a church, with a window opening into the church so that she could observe services, and another window to the outside world where people could come for advice and spiritual direction. She had a maid, Alice, who did her cleaning and cooking.

Julian lived in a time when visions were both normal and expected. Her writings are about her visions, or showings, as they were called at that time. As a young woman, probably from a privileged class since she could both read and write, Julian prayed for three signs or gifts: an understanding of the Passion of Christ; a bodily illness that would show her an understanding of death; and three wounds—a wound of contrition, a wound of compassion, and a wound of longing for God.

Stories of three wishes fill fairy-tale books. For Julian, the tale became reality. At the age of 30, the year that she requested, Julian developed an illness that paralyzed her lower body and then her upper body so that her breathing was giving out. She was so close to death that she was administered the last rites of the Church. Within six days, Julian fully recovered. During her illness, as a crucifix was held before her, she saw blood flowing from under the crown on Christ's head. Julian saw 16 visions in just over a 24-hour period, which constitute the text of her book.

She wrote her book twice. The first writing, known as the Short Text, immediately followed her visions. The Long Text, written years later, includes interpretations or learnings she gleaned from 20 years of searching and "listening" for meanings of these episodes.

How does a medieval woman sealed up in a cell next to a church serve as a model for women entering the twenty-first century?

Foremost, following her visions, experience is primary for Julian. She struggles to reconcile her experience with the Church's teachings. Medieval church teachings pictured God as vengeful to sinners. People are condemned to eternal punishment. Her discourse on sin and forgiveness runs almost 35 of the Long Text's 86 chapters. The answer that she is given is one of pure compassion.

‹ Wrath does not exist in God but only in us.

‹ God's forgiveness is not outside but within
  ourselves.

‹ It is our own self-hatred that must be transformed.

Julian sounds more like a modern-day psychiatrist than a medieval teacher.

Julian often walked a tightrope with her teachings. She was supported by the Church and was required to espouse its doctrine or be accused of heresy and risk condemnation. Yet she wrote as her vision was revealed to her. Indeed, some have labeled her words heresy, others a testament of sublime faith. When she asked God why sin even exists, God replied, in what has probably become the most famous saying of her book, "It behoved that there should be sin: but all shall be well, and all shall be well, and all manner of things shall be well."[4]

In the Short Text, the first book about her visions, Julian merely describes the visions. Her strength and conviction emerge in the Long Text, where she gently holds her own against Church doctrine. In a society where the Church dominates all aspects of one's life, Julian is a woman to be admired.

Julian is loved and admired by modern women because of her understanding of the feminine side of God. She declares that "as truly as God is our Father, so truly is God our Mother" (Long Text 59). Steeped in the traditional church language of the Trinity, she is nonetheless as likely to place "our Mother" in the second position as she is to name Christ. In fact, her devotion to the motherhood of God finds its home in the Trinity. She is able to state that with three entities for God there is no single concept that describes the divine. The Trinity is able to free her rather than confine her doctrinally.

"I saw the blessed Trinity working. I saw that there were these three attributes: fatherhood, motherhood, and lordship—all in one God.

"In our Mother, Christ, we grow and develop; in his mercy he reforms and restores us; through his passion, death, and resurrection he has united us to our being. . . . In our merciful Mother we have reformation and re-newal."[5]

Christian women today who have embraced femi-nist language for God find themselves dismissed or out-right condemned by "orthodox" church leaders. Within every major denomination, groups have organized in backlash to reinstate traditional male-language-only for God. Imagine what Julian must have encountered in her day.

As a mystic, Julian advises her followers to meditate. Her words are not her own but ones that have been given to her. "He spoke to me thus: 'Pray inwardly, although there seems to be no savour in it, yet it is profitable. Pray inwardly, even though you think you cannot.'

"God is nearer to us than our own soul," she writes. "For He is the ground in whom our soul stands."[6]

Union with God will bring ultimate knowledge of life's meaning. This supreme teaching is found in the final chapter of the Long Text: "And from the time that it was revealed, I desired many times to know in what was our Lord's meaning. And fifteen years after and more . . . it was said: What, do you wish to know your Lord's meaning in this thing? Know it well, love was His meaning. Who revealed it to you? Love. What did he reveal to you? Love.

Why does he reveal it to you? For Love. Remain in this, and you will know more of the same. But you will never know different, without end."[7]

The word *self-esteem* is not found in the vocabulary of a medieval writer; even the concept would be foreign. Yet Julian of Norwich exhibited traits that we look for today.

She was grounded in the reality of both her visions (God said to her, "Know it well, it was no hallucination which you saw today.")[8] and her life as an anchoress. She set goals for herself—the first to have an experience with the divine—and continued to live a disciplined life of meditation, writing, teaching, and advising. Her goals were centered in her life's purpose. She was able to establish clear boundaries with others, including the Church upon which she had made herself dependent. There is no doubt that her life was integrated with her beliefs and that her integrity was unquestioned. Her centered life made her sought after by her contemporaries and admired by generations to come.

By the middle of the fourteenth century, the Holy Church was persecuting individuals and groups who placed experience over doctrine. Julian was spared because she couched her revelations within church language and at a church site. Freedom to experience divinity for oneself rather than within the confines of orthodoxy is the greatest threat to established religion. The Inquisition would not be far in the future.

Meera of India

Just as Julian of Norwich functioned as an independent woman within the context of her medieval Christian culture, so Meera is grounded in her sixteenth-century Hindu culture. Her adoration of Krishna is the center point of her life. At the same time, Meera challenges basic concepts of life as dictated for women in her era.

Meera is a poet and singer of songs. It is her songs that have been passed down and finally translated for us by Shama Futehally[9] through a grant by the Arts Council of Great Britain.

While Meera was born in 1498 during a period of Muslim rule, her family and the surrounding countryside of Rajastham were predominantly Hindu. The immediate world of Meera was traditional. Her family was in the caste of *kshatriya*, rulers and soldiers below the priests but above the merchant caste. Obedience and chastity were hallmarks of womanhood. Patriarchy was so entrenched that a local custom decreed that all women commit mass suicide if defeat were inevitable during battle, rather than fall into enemy hands and be "dishonored."

Meera's marriage in 1516 was political. The yoking of one clan to another would help forge unity between two clans and strengthen the position against the Muslims.

It was prior to this marriage that Meera claimed her true allegiance to Krishna, the eighth incarnation of the

Hindu god Vishnu. Hindus often select one of many incarnations that are most meaningful to them or to their household. The first duty of a new wife was to worship the family deity. In the case of Meera's in-laws, this was Shakti. Meera began immediately to disregard custom in her new marriage by refusing to worship her husband's family god.

Meera was now a princess but had little regard for social status or privilege that comes with royalty. Meera mingled with people from other classes, including men and strangers. Her worship of Krishna took her to the temple where she broke custom for a princess by dancing and singing in public.

Meera became part of what was known as the bhakti movement, which originated around the sixth century in southern India. The movement grew extensively during the Middle Ages, so generalizing it is difficult. However, it tends to be a mystical movement where devotees are not so bound to traditional values. Its central message is love (Julian's final message), and it is often characterized by egalitarianism and liberation.

Even though Meera's husband died just three years after their marriage, his family persecuted her in order to defend its honor against her rejection of its privilege and social caste. Her insubordination as a woman was more than they could bear. Tradition has it that even though they tried to kill her by poisoning, Meera was unchangeable. Finally, she set off on her own travels around India, writing and singing songs to Krishna, the god in whom she had found love. Rather than stay in one place, as did Julian of Norwich, she wandered as a devotee to deepen her spiritual self and share her devotion and message of love with others.

According to her songs, Meera's union with the divine is fleeting: "On a sudden, the sight./Your look of light stills all, stills all" (Song 22). Yet, she waits, removing herself from her center so Krishna can occupy that space.

What can we learn from a woman who wandered the countryside half a world away four centuries ago? We can learn to find meaning within ourselves rather than from status and wealth. We can learn not to trade our souls for security. Listen to the first three stanzas of Song 13:

> *Girls! Come form a ring.*
> *We'll dance,*
> *we'll turn away*
> *from playing at what the elders say;*
> *we'll look within*
> *not go away*
> *not go and give ourselves away*
> > *to homes*
> > *that are strange*
> > *to the soul.*

We learn that following our instinctive voice may bring us judgment and rejection but that the internal rewards are worth it. We learn that women standing up to stultifying patriarchy is not a new feminist phenomenon of the 1970s and later, but history replaying itself over the centuries.

Meera learned that communication with her god, Krishna, could be direct and that inaccessible rituals and scriptures were not necessary. We can learn to value our own experience just as she did hers.

Meera may have been condemned by the royal family that she abandoned, but her courage and the beauty of her songs have made her one of India's most beloved saints. She inspired many, including Gandhi, with her distinctive mystical and feminist spiritual songs.

Peace Pilgrim

A modern woman who looks just like you or me— one we can relate to. Well, perhaps.

If we can conceive of ourselves walking back and forth across the United States seven times to talk to individuals and groups about peace, both inner peace and world peace.

Mildred Ryder was born in New Jersey around 1908. By the time she was 16, she was a senior in high school with the highest grade in her class. Her family was peace-oriented—her ancestors had left Germany to escape militarism. Discussions of peace dominated her household.

Ryder's family belonged to no church, and she received no formal religious training. As her spiritual life deepened she claimed only Universal Truth as her spiritual home. What impresses me most about her spiritual life was that the teachings that she learned from within herself are those of all religions. She kept asking questions and waiting patiently for answers. Her time of meditation was walking in the woods in "receptive silence."

After graduation, Ryder worked, bought luxuries, dressed in the flapper styles of the era, wore excessive makeup, danced, and partied. None of this satisfied her.

"I discovered that making money was easy. I had been led to believe that money and possessions could ensure me a life of happiness and peace of mind. So that was the path I pursued. In the second place, I discovered that making money and spending it foolishly was completely meaningless. I knew that this was not what I was here for, but at that time I didn't know exactly what I was here for."[10]

When Ryder was about 30, her deep search for a meaningful way of life led her to pray that her life would be one of service. She began to "live to give what I could, instead of to get what I could, and I entered a new and wonderful world."[11] She simplified her living and began doing for others. She experienced a great peace.

Ryder experienced a 15-year internal conflict before she set out on her pilgrimage. The struggle occurred between what she called the lower self and the higher self, or the self-centered nature and the God-centered nature. During these years her marriage dissolved and she became more active in the peace movement, working as a legislative lobbyist for peace in Washington, D.C. She continued to simplify her life and take her walks in receptive silence looking for answers.

She describes her first experience of true inner peace: "I was out walking in the early morning. All of a sudden I felt very uplifted, more uplifted than I had ever been. I remember I knew timelessness and spacelessness and lightness. I did not seem to be walking on the earth. There were no people or even animals around, but every flower, every bush, every tree seemed to wear a halo. There was a light emanation around everything and flecks of gold fell like slanted rain through the air. . . . The most important part of it was the realization of the oneness of all creation."[12]

After this experience, Ryder stopped eating animal flesh and even picking flowers. The unity of all creation had become a reality for her.

Always an adventurer, Ryder was the first woman to hike the Appalachian Trail. Toward the end of this 2,000-mile hike she experienced an inner vision of the map of the United States with lines extending from city to city. She saw herself in the navy blue pants and tunic top that would become her uniform. She would walk across the country, following the lines that she envisioned, in her new outfit.

On January 1, 1953, she set out on her pilgrimage as Peace Pilgrim. She would "walk until given shelter, fast until given food." She never missed more than four meals in a row. "Aren't people good!" she would exclaim.[13]

It was the era of the Korean War and McCarthyism. The FBI targeted her as a communist and followed her and harassed her family. At that time she dropped her former name completely and used only Peace Pilgrim for the rest of her life. Many of her family and former friends rejected her. Her brother-in-law explained that "she was no longer the Mildred they knew and therefore beyond their comprehension."[14]

Once she found inner peace, like Meera and many others, she was not afraid to risk disapproval. She talks about walking down a city street in midafternoon.

> *Hundreds of neatly dressed human beings with*
> *pale or painted faces hurried in rather orderly*
> *lines to and from their places of employment. I, in*
> *my faded shirt and well-worn slacks, walked*
> *among them. The rubber soles of my soft canvas*
> *shoes moved noiselessly along beside the clatter of*
> *trim, tight shoes with stiltlike heels. In the poorer*
> *section I was tolerated. In the wealthier section*
> *some glances seemed a bit startled and some were*
> *disdainful.*

SELF AND SOUL

> *On both sides of us as we walked were displayed*
> *the things we can buy if we are willing to stay in*
> *the orderly lines day after day, year after year. . . .*
> *Thousands of things are displayed—and yet my*
> *friends, the most valuable are missing. Freedom is*
> *not displayed, nor health, nor happiness, nor*
> *peace of mind. To obtain these things, my friends,*
> *you too may need to escape from the orderly lines*
> *and risk being looked upon disdainfully.*[15]

Her message to the world was summarized in one sentence, which she never changed: "This is the way of peace: Overcome evil with good, falsehood with truth, and hatred with love."

Peace Pilgrim developed steps for achieving inner peace. She calls it a do-it-yourself project. "There is no glimpse of the light without walking the path. You can't get it from anyone else, nor can you give it to anyone."[16] Peace Pilgrim set down the path she used to achieve inner peace in a booklet called "Steps toward Inner Peace," which she passed out as she walked.

After Peace Pilgrim's death—or transition, as she would have called it—in 1981, five of her friends put together a book of her life and work using quotes that they could find from taped speeches, letters, and articles. Today, *Peace Pilgrim: Her Life and Work in Her Own Words*, has been translated into 6 different languages, and her little "Steps toward Inner Peace" booklet into 21.

Following Peace Pilgrim's example, all books are distributed free to anyone who requests. Donations have kept these friends of Peace Pilgrim busy into multiple printings. (For your copy, write: Friends of Peace Pilgrim, 43480 Cedar Avenue, Hemet, CA 92544.)

Three women found themselves by looking deep within. Once they knew who they were, they never compromised themselves. Their goals for living stemmed from this inner knowing, discovered through meditation and spiritual awareness.

Many more models exist for us, and yet we may never hear about them because their stories were not considered significant enough to be recorded. We need to claim as many as we can.

Exercises: Points to Ponder

1. What women are role models for you? Are any from your spiritual tradition? Take time and read their stories.

2. In what ways can stories like these be helpful to you? Write your own story. How does it read?

10

On Becoming a Mystic: Creating a New Reality

"Remember no one can make you feel inferior without your consent."

—Eleanor Roosevelt[1]

❧

Desire for Change

"I want to be like that." This pervasive thought enters my mind every time I read about the mystics.

No, I don't want to be sealed up in a room attached to the wall of a medieval church. I don't want to wander around India writing songs or walk across North America with nothing in my pockets but a comb, toothbrush, and pen. What I want is the same inner assurance that Julian of Norwich, Meera of India, Peace Pilgrim, and many more people like them exhibit. As someone once advised, "Seek not to imitate the saints; seek what they sought."

I have shown videos of Peace Pilgrim to various groups. People who sincerely want to deepen their lives are fascinated; others think that she must have been bizarre at best, off her rocker at worst. One woman exclaimed, "She really knew who she was and didn't let anyone or anything stop her from being that."

Peace Pilgrim called her devotion to inner peace a do-it-yourself project. Only your desire to live a spiritually centered life will lead you to do it. Our present culture is not helpful. Many current values contradict the principles of both self-esteem and spirituality for women. Society's values lead to low self-esteem because they are based on comparison—having more than, being more successful than, being more beautiful than. No matter how much of these you achieve, someone else will always have or be more than you.

How, then, to "do it yourself"?

The following pages outline practical steps that we can take to enhance our inner esteem and find peace at the same time.

Practice Meditation Regularly

Do you have regular communication with your spiritual center? Regular communication with your spiritual center, or God, is important (for more information, see "The Practice of Meditation" on page 50). Saint Theresa of Avila immersed herself in contemplation (the sixteenth-century term for what we know today as meditation) for more than 15 years before she experienced the visions or raptures that redirected her life. We do not need visions and rapture. What we need is a peaceful soul to take into everyday life.

Regular quieting of the mind from the stresses and busyness of everyday activity helps us keep a healthy perspective on life. Make sure that it is a part of your day.

Write Your Own Mission Statement

Why are you living your life the way you are? A mission statement gives the reason why something exists. Businesses have them; hospitals have them; nonprofit organizations have them. I suggest that we each have one.

❲ In a quiet setting, perhaps where you meditate every day, set aside a half-hour.

❲ Take a blank piece of paper and write at the top, "I am here on this Earth to. . . " Write down anything that comes to mind. Statements that I see frequently include:

> *"I am here on this Earth to raise my children*
> *to be physically and emotionally healthy."*

ON BECOMING A MYSTIC: CREATING A NEW REALITY

"*I am here on this Earth to provide for my family.*"

"*I am here on this Earth to enjoy life and the beauty of the world.*"

"*I am here on this Earth to form loving and caring relationships with others.*"

"*I am here on this Earth to discover who I am and develop my potential to the fullest.*"

"*I am here on this Earth to help ABC company develop a safer and more reliable product for consumers.*"

"*I am here on this Earth to help heal others through the medical profession.*"

Think of all areas of your life. Do they move toward fulfilling a life purpose? Write it down.

Be sure to include the work that you perform outside the home. Is your job fulfilling your life's mission, or is it just a way to make money? You would be surprised at what a difference your attitude about work is if you feel that it has a meaningful purpose. Approaching work as another sacred area of life enhances your feeling of total wholeness about yourself.

One of Buddhism's precepts of the Eightfold Path is right livelihood. According to Buddha, spiritual progress is impossible if what we do eight or more hours a day works against it. Therefore, be certain that you engage in life-enhancing work. Professions that destroy life will consume your soul as well.

I have never seen mission statements that people write (and I have groups do this on a regular basis) that say they are here on this earth to amass enough money to retire early, to party every weekend, to try to put the business down the street out of existence, to show so-and-so that they are wrong, or to create hostility with their in-laws. As Peace Pilgrim would say, getting the believing and living together is the harder part.

❝ After you have listed what you believe your reason to exist is, complete the next sentence fragment: "To accomplish this I must..." Again, write down everything that comes to mind. Don't worry about your grammar and syntax. You are not working on a manuscript to submit to your English teacher. You are developing reasons for living your life according to its purpose. Usually, the answers come tumbling out with amazing speed.

> "I must set aside more time for my partner, for my children, for..."
>
> "I must concentrate on my tasks at work and ignore the negative office gossip."
>
> "I must set aside a time every morning for meditation."
>
> "I must concentrate on a healthier lifestyle, eating better and exercising regularly."

❝ A good format for this part of your mission statement is to break these statements down into three sections:

> *What do I need to eliminate from my life to make room for my purpose?*
>
> *What do I need to add to make this kind of life happen?*
>
> *What do I need to learn in order to accomplish my purpose?*

When asked to write a purpose for their lives, many people look at me blankly. "This is really hard," one woman cried out. If you have never thought of your life in these terms, it is indeed hard. But you will find it beneficial. It will help you evaluate how you spend your time. Do I really need to serve on that committee? How can I free up Tuesday evenings to help my daughter's Girl Scout leader? Getting that degree is important; how can I make it happen?

Set up a plan to fulfill your goals. Post these somewhere where you will be reminded of them.

Take your mission statement out and rework it every six months. Life circumstances and priorities change. Children grow and move out. Work evolves. Your personal life has its own ebb and flow. As your purpose emerges with different emphases, what you need to do to accomplish it will change. You are writing life goals and how you can achieve them.

SELF AND SOUL

Cultivate a Positive Attitude toward Living

What is your philosophy of life? Do you believe that the cup is half-full or half-empty? Is life intrinsically good or inherently evil? Are problems and challenges opportunities for learning in disguise or life's bum rap?

I know that when I am mired in the middle of a personal crisis and someone smiles and says, "Remember that every cloud has a silver lining," my receptivity to this advice is hardly favorable. But I have learned that a positive outlook on life is key to a positive sense of self.

Most of my workshops begin with an amazing technique to prove the power of our thoughts, both positive and negative. A volunteer stands before the group and repeats to herself 10 times, "I am a weak and unworthy person." I ask her to internalize this statement while she repeats it. Then I ask her to raise her dominant arm straight in front of her with her fist clenched and resist my force. It has never failed. I easily push her arm down to her side.

Since we never leave anything negatively, she next repeats to herself 10 times, "I am a strong and worthy person," again internalizing the message. After this sequence, I ask her to once again lift her arm. She holds her arm strong and fast.

Seeing is not always believing. Therefore, all participants are invited to find a partner and repeat the exercise, exchanging roles as they go. They experience the power of both their own and another's thoughts for themselves.

I am only five feet three inches tall. I have successfully used this exercise with men who are six feet five inches tall. It works!

After this demonstration, I do not have to spend great amounts of time explaining the necessity for positive thinking. If we can make our arms go up and down through positive or negative thoughts, think of what we can do with the rest of our lives.

Repeat positive affirmations. This has become routine practice in self-esteem circles. Putting messages on the bathroom mirror that proclaim, "I am capable in what I do" feels silly to many people, and they are quickly removed if company suddenly shows up. Yet they are beginning steps that you can take to rewrite the subconscious.

Think about your friends. Who are the positive ones? Spend more time with them so that their influence can rub off on you. There are people that I call energy givers and others that I label energy drainers. I have started limiting my contact with those who leave me emotionally drained after a visit. I'm not talking about friends who are undergoing genuine adversity. I'm talking about people who are always in crisis, who thrive on crisis, but never take steps to move out of crisis.

Stay upbeat and positive. Like attracts like. Soon you will find yourself surrounded by joyful people, and the negative ones will drift elsewhere.

Being a positive person is a choice that you make.

We all know people who have led difficult lives yet are still joyful. Likewise, we each can point to individuals who are always negative even though their lives have been relatively stress-free and successful by most standards.

I called my sister-in-law last week to inquire about her dying mother. Elizabeth has watched her mother slowly deteriorate from an Alzheimer-type disease for the last 11 years. As I write this, she is in a coma close to death. Elizabeth and Sam struggled for years to combine two families with their marriage, which was the second for both. The five children are grown and gone. Now, with Elizabeth in her late fifties and Sam in his early sixties, they finally have their dream home in the mountains of Colorado. Elizabeth said to me, "Sam and I have realized that we are in the best time of our lives, and we will do everything possible to remain joyful under all these circumstances. We just will not let this situation pull us down."

Or as poet Maya Angelou's grandmother used to say, "What you're supposed to do when you don't like a thing is change it. If you can't change it, change the way you think about it. Don't complain."[2]

Eliminate Negative Influences in Your Life

What pulls you down? A study was conducted by the *Philadelphia Inquirer* in 1995 that showed that people who watched local news telecasts regularly viewed their neighborhoods as more dangerous than those who did not. Crime statistics revealed that the perception of crime was far higher than the reality for those television news viewers.

I believe that much of the negativity in today's world stems from overstimulation of our senses with negative images.

Our television walked out of our house with one of our sons when he left home for his first apartment. It was never replaced. After a few years of increased serenity, I realize that I have never seen Rwandans butchering one another (although I keep myself abreast of world events through newspapers.) I did not watch any of the O. J. Simpson trial. I do not observe who-slept-with-whom scenarios on daytime talk shows. I am not bombarded with fictional violence and unruly behavior on prime time. My mind is not insulted by lobotomized sitcoms. My senses are no longer being assaulted with negative images. What a difference it has made in my disposition.

Just eliminating commercials from my life changed how I view the world. I realized recently that I no longer think of the average woman as five feet seven inches tall, thin, with long blond hair, like those parading across television commercials, soap operas, and sitcoms. I see the women in the grocery store as not only average but also the norm.

You may not want to put your television on the front stoop for the garbage collector, but be assured that what you watch affects you very much. Advertisers spend millions to make a difference in how you think. Be selective in what you watch. Choose programs that do not stereotype women, degrade them, or abuse them, even in the name of humor. Enjoy and learn from the wonderful educational shows. Just press the off button when trashier shows appear.

One psychologist says that when patients come to her for depression, the first thing she tells them is not to watch television or read the newspaper for one month. Negative images bombard us constantly through media and pull us down before we realize it. We can only block so many before we buy into the negative message about life that they convey.

I grow weary listening to debates concerning violence and sex on television. Since I have never met anyone who thinks that violence and sex belong on television, I can't figure out why the shows still exist. If everyone who complained simply turned off their televisions, there would be no negative shows left to complain about. Remember Angelou's grandmother: Stop complaining; do something.

Think about other negative influences that surround you. Many magazines written for women consumers portray the same stereotypes that give us inadequate feelings about ourselves. Does looking at the covers of *Glamour* or *Cosmopolitan* make you feel fat, mousey-haired, and poorly dressed? They may. That is how many advertisers who support these periodicals sell their wares to you so that you can "beautify" yourself. Once you know that real beauty comes from within, you will be less likely to purchase unnecessary items just because someone promotes them. Your healthy, whole self is sexually attractive (notice I did not say thin—healthy and thin are not exchangeable terms). You radiate a warmth that others want. You have beauty that is more than skin-deep.

If magazines make you feel inadequate, cancel your subscriptions and spend the money on something that energizes you.

What about the books you read? What types of women are portrayed? It might be fun to escape into a romance novel, but those portraying a femme fatale waiting for a hero to come rescue her from danger only reinforce the weak image of women. Many newer books have strong women heroines. Read books that portray the kind of woman that you are striving to become. You might find the works of Alice Walker, Anna Quinlen, Toni Morrison, Amy Tan, Margaret Atwood, or Anne Tyler inspiring.

Eliminate the negative habit of worry. The word itself has a negative root—it is derived from an old Anglo-Saxon word meaning "to choke."[3] Every time you worry, imagine that someone is putting his hands around your neck choking you. That is what you do to yourself when you engage in worry. Worry is something that you do about situations over which you have no control. If you can change something, do it. If you can't, accept that for the time being while you work for change. Just don't worry.

My son Ben set out across the country with his 1982 Volvo station wagon loaded down with his personal belongings. He doesn't know where he will end up. He plans to travel and sightsee for six weeks before he reaches the West Coast. I could sit every day and worry that he will run out of money or get sick. My worry would not change the reality of his trip one bit. Instead, I have chosen to wish him well and look forward to hearing about every adventure that he has along the way. If trouble should spring up, we will deal with it then. In the meantime, happy traveling! (An update: Yes, Ben's car did break down in Colorado. Yes, he was robbed in Sacramento, California. But guess what? He made it to Oregon, found a job and a place to live, and is loving life!)

When you realize that you are worrying, short periods of meditation can be helpful. Clear your mind and picture the situation at its best. Then set about some other task totally unrelated with a clear and relaxed mind.

If you find yourself lying awake at night stewing over a problem, repeat a mantra or a piece that you have memorized for meditation over and over in your mind. Your mind cannot handle the inspirational piece and your worry at the same time. With time, you will train yourself to begin this recitation as soon as a worry comes. Sleep will once again return.

Eliminate other negative emotions. The destructive nature of fear and anger were addressed in chapter 6. Continue to work on healing the incidents that trigger these emotions in you. Remember that your anger at others destroys you, not them.

Deal with the negative people in your life. Does your spouse put you down? Your parents? Ask them to stop, and if they do not, seek counseling together. If the other party won't participate, go alone. Often, time apart from negative people is required to gather strength to deal with them in the future. Sometimes the separation must be permanent.

If anyone in your life is physically, sexually, or extremely emotionally abusive, leave immediately. You can look at mending the relationship from a distance for a while, but never, ever allow anyone to abuse you in any way. Shelters for abused women are within reach of almost all women in the United States today. Professional help is there for you. Utilize it. They will help you find housing and financial support. And good luck.

One of my good friends is a breast cancer survivor. She underwent a double mastectomy, chemotherapy, and radiation—a year and a half of horror. Following her experience she joined a support group. Recently, I asked her if she still attended. "No," she said. "They were so negative about everything. That's not what I need. I need to be surrounded by positive people at this time in my life." Good advice. How sad for the remaining women in the group whose lives have already been difficult enough without pulling down one another weekly.

Work for Social Justice

What do you do to make the world a better place? It seems like an overwhelming, impossible task. It's hard to believe that one person—you—could make a difference. It's also easy to become cynical today. Despite the tremendous gains made in women's lives over the last 20 years, we still see our friends (or ourselves) passed over for promotion because of gender; some have only low-paying service job options; some are treated in a patronizing fashion by doctors, sales clerks, and others; some are sexually harassed as they walk down the street; and some suffer battering at the hands of their spouses.

It is easy to name continued injustices to women. But what are you doing about them? You may not be able to change some situations today. You can, however, continue to work for future improvement.

❰ Letter-writing campaigns to legislators make a difference.

❰ Volunteering at a rape crisis center or a battered women's shelter improves lives, while at the same time, puts you in the center of what's happening for women in your community.

❮ Vote. Know where your state legislator, congress-person, or senator stands on women's issues. Work for those who support women.

Becoming a mystic is not withdrawal from daily life, pretending that life is a breeze. It is totally integrating our lives, including the voting booth and the bank, and being in harmony with a joyful and centered spirit.

When you are working for change, you will lose the feeling of helplessness, and you will be making a difference for others.

At the conclusion of a year's monthly gatherings on self-esteem and spirituality for survivors of domestic violence, Liz mused, "What I've learned this year is that I really need to feel that God is within me in order for my self-esteem to stay at a good level. After all, if I have that, I'll be able to keep everything else we've talked about. My relatives and friends keep wanting to fix me up with other men, but I just tell them, I have to get me right first. This year has been for healing me and getting all of these principles to work for me."

Liz is right. Her value must come from within. The rest will follow. Discovery of the spiritual center will lead to internal freedom and confidence.

11

Migration to Joy

"You don't get to choose how you're going to die, or when. You can only decide how you're going to live. Now!"

—Joan Baez[1]

❧

The Quest

What is it that makes us go looking for ourselves everywhere but where we are? In the last 30 years we have moved to and out of California, set up housekeeping in communes, and abandoned our faith heritage to climb the Himalayas and follow gurus of every ilk. We have hung crystals from the rearview mirror, channeled, huddled in sweat lodges, smoked pot and peace pipes, chanted, drummed, and danced. We have studied transcendental meditation, supported others and been supported ourselves, rebirthed and parented inner children, listened actively, emoted, joined encounter groups, and affirmed.

Yet the quest goes on.

Have we been too busy packing for our next llama trip (too weary now to carry our own baggage) to realize how empty our inner selves remain and what that emptiness does to us?

It matters not whether we were one of the many women who sought meaning from baking seven-grain bread in a braid with a crusty finish, or one who tried to find satisfaction in the best sales record of the corporation. No matter what we did that was of excellence, the high lasted only briefly. The nagging question, "How good are we really?" eventually resurfaced.

This emptiness manifested as low self-esteem and plagued us like the deer tick. Only a tiny bite wreaks havoc on our entire system, causing first just a rash, but finally leaving us almost paralyzed with rheumatic symptoms of Lyme disease: fatigued, achy, with no zest for life.

What is merely a dark night of the soul for some is for many women a way of life—never venturing out into light, remaining hidden behind the veil that society has draped around their very being. The veil that reminds them that they can be smart, but not too smart; that certain dimensions are called for in their bodies and anything else is not acceptable; that giving, not receiving, is their trade; that self-denial has nothing to do with false ego and everything to do with providing doormats for others to walk upon.

The quest goes on. Until one day, just as a bird begins circling above the earth in preparation for her flight to the climate best for her survival, the soul begins to break free. If the legs are not tethered too fast to everyday pegs, the migration is possible.

The migration to joy.

A Glimpse of Joy

We've all experienced it at some time. Perhaps it was while watching a sunset, walking along the beach, climbing a mountain, holding a baby, cuddling in a lover's arms. It may not have lasted long, but you remember it. That instant when time stood still and the goodness of life filled your being. During that time, no bills begged to be paid, no illness wracked your body, no deadlines jangled in your mind, no daughter came crying with a scraped knee, no unemployed son came home to live. Stress was obsolete.

Oh, to stay in that moment forever.

Gifts of grace, religious folk call these moments. They are gifts that may be given freely, but we can set the stage for their appearance and help them last longer than a few fleeting seconds. These flickers of joy can lengthen to a steady flame. We can do more than glimpse joy in special settings. We can live it in the midst of bills, sickness, injury, and crisis. All we need to do is decide to begin the flight.

Self and soul—a commitment to one is a commitment to the other. A commitment to both is a determination to experience joy and peace in your life on a regular basis. You can make this happen. It is a choice to take the necessary steps or to place this book back on the shelf and go on with living life in all of the dreariness that you perceive it to be. Why not wake up each day knowing that your journey has a destination of "permanent joy"?

We are used to talking about happiness in the conditional sense: If only I received a salary raise, then I could be happy. If only I found the perfect man, then I would know joy. If only, if only, if only. The elevation of mood that accompanies good things in life is real, but it is temporary. Expenses rise to meet the new salary level. The perfect man, in fact, snores. What goes up must come down. Happiness has an opposite. Joy does not.

The joy that comes from within the self is not subject to the ups and downs of life. It emerges from a well-nurtured soul.

I used to be quite cautious and cynical about this subject. After all, aren't these sentiments just platitudes used to hold people in their place? "You can be content in an abusive relationship, as long as your soul is at peace." "Learn to put up with the sexual harassment of your boss—you know in your heart what is right." "Don't worry about your bills—the Lord will provide."

Remember that Rosa Parks had an abiding faith, but that did not prevent her from remaining seated at the front of a bus rather than moving dutifully toward the back. Mahatma Gandhi's soul was quite well, but after he was kicked off a train because of the color of his skin, he set out to work for equality for all Indians. The apostle Paul wrote that he learned to be content whether in prison or free, yet when the doors of the jail sprang open, he departed quickly.

It takes a very strong soul and sense of self to walk out of a bad situation, perhaps not even knowing where you might sleep or work the next day—living on faith that your inner voice, your God within, your Christ consciousness will lead you to the right destination.

I am no longer cautious about the use of faith to traverse unknown paths. In fact, I believe that it is the only way to go. Instead, I am cautious about those who use faith against others. They are the ones afraid of our inner strength. It just might change their status quo. I am also cautious when we are intimidated by admonitions such as the ones listed above. Then we have not learned to listen to our inner wisdom.

Leap of Faith

When the season of your life is right, your migration will begin—the migration into the very depth of your being. No lead goose will come to gather you into a flock. You begin the journey when you are ready.

One day you will wake up and decide that you want more from life. You want a profound peace that carries you through each day and all of your responsibilities. You desire something greater than a wrinkle-free face and flab-free body. You crave serenity amidst the day's turbulence. Not only do you yearn for it, you are ready to act to make it happen.

No wonder it is called a leap of faith. It is one journey that you begin not knowing how you will arrive at the destination. Road maps are available to get you started—meditation, goal-setting, self-care, service—but each turn in the road brings new surprises. New wonders and struggles await you. Are you ready? Friends may change; career changes may be necessary; old habits may need to be replaced with new ones.

The inner urgings are strong enough. You are ready to take flight.

Entering the Garden of Joy

The Secret Garden is one of my favorite childhood stories. Its release as a movie gave me an opportunity to attend a matinee by myself, get a large container of pop-corn and a soda, and settle in for an afternoon delight. *The Secret Garden* is an enchanting story of unhappiness transformed into joy when a few children venture into a secret inner sanctum, a garden locked away and named off-limits by those who think that life should be proper and serious. It is in this space that the children taste, smell, and see; feel the richness of the earth; listen to the wisdom of the birds and deer; and see the changing seasons. In this arena, old wounds are healed, the lame walk, and grief turns into joy. The secret of that garden is the daring of one little girl to do the forbidden—steal the key, turn it, and enter the unknown. It never occurred to her not to explore this interior world; nothing would stop her.

Dare to do the same: Turn the key and enter the inner sanctum of your soul where old wounds can be healed and grief can turn into joy.

Trappist monk Thomas Merton wrote, "The only true joy on earth is to escape from the prison of our own false self, and enter by love into union with the Life Who dwells and sings within the essence of every creature and in the core of our own souls."[2]

The Joy of Self-Esteem

Possessing high self-esteem means living life in a new way. It is no longer self-centered; instead, it is self-fulfilled. It means not being bound by others' approval but being secure in oneself. It is not a state of "happy-happy" all the time; instead, it is a quiet contentedness even at those times when we feel down.

Let us review once again the principles of self-esteem found in chapter 3.

1. People with high self-esteem operate out of a sense of reality rather than fantasy. They are aware of both their internal feelings and external situations. Plainly, a person cannot hide in religious platitudes and be in touch with reality.

2. People who operate with high self-esteem know how to alter their reality favorably through realistic goals and purposes for their lives. They are not stuck in a situation.

3. People with high self-esteem know how to establish boundaries and stand up for themselves. They are not used by others.

4. People who appreciate themselves live their lives with integrity. Their inner, spiritual life is integrated with their everyday life and reflected in high standards of behavior.

Make no mistake. It feels good to live like this. Inner joy and authentic self-esteem resonate with one another. Developing self-esteem is a spiritual process.

Over the years I have worked on my own self-esteem issues. I did not make significant progress until I decided to make developing my spiritual life a number one priority. As I sat and listened to my inner voice, I became more confident in myself. Self-esteem was an outgrowth of a spiritual quest.

My journey is hardly over. I know that it may take many more years before I remain joyful through all situations. But the depth of joy in my life continues to increase. Confidence in myself continues to grow. I am thankful.

As Peace Pilgrim proclaimed, "Who could know God and not be joyous?"[3]

Notes

*All Bible verses are quoted from the
New Revised Standard Version.*

Chapter 1

1. Peggy Anderson, comp., *Great Quotes from Great Women* (Lombard, Ill.: Celebrating Excellence, 1992), 86.

2. Christiane Northrup, *Women's Bodies, Women's Wisdom* (New York: Bantam, 1994), 435.

3. Hillary Rodham Clinton, *It Takes a Village* (New York: Simon and Schuster, 1996).

4. For a more elaborate discussion on characteristics of low self-esteem, see Paul Hauck, *Overcoming the Rating Game* (Louisville: John Knox Press, 1991).

5. These statistics were quoted and given out at a 1993 workshop on self-esteem produced by CareerTrack.

6. Barbara Arnwine, "Bum Raps, Bubba, and Affirmative Action," interview in *On the Issues* (fall 1995): 54.

7. William Appleton, quoted in Linda Sanford and Mary Donovan, *Women and Self-Esteem* (New York: Penguin, 1984), 7.

8. Hauck, *Overcoming the Rating Game*, 8.

9. Nathaniel Brandon, *The Six Pillars of Self-Esteem* (New York: Bantam, 1994), 27.

10. Sanford and Donovan, *Women and Self-Esteem*, 7.

Chapter 2

1. Carol Flinders, *Enduring Grace* (New York: HarperCollins, 1993), 223.

2. Huston Smith, *The World's Great Religions* (New York: HarperCollins, 1991), 5.

3. Gerda Lerner, *The Creation of Feminist Consciousness* (New York: Oxford University Press, 1993). See, especially, chapter 7, "One Thousand Years of Feminist Bible Criticism."

4. L. Christenson, *The Christian Family* (Minneapolis: Bethany House, 1970), 47, 53.

5. Nathaniel Brandon, *The Six Pillars of Self-Esteem* (New York: Bantam, 1994), 148.

6. Thomas Jackson, ed. *The Works of John Wesley*, Vol. 9 (London: John Mason, 1829), 429.

Chapter 3

1. Rosalie Maggio, comp., *Beacon Book of Quotations by Women* (Boston: Beacon Press, 1992), 283.

2. Portia Nelson, *There's a Hole in My Sidewalk* (Hillsboro, Oreg.: Beyond Words Publishing, 1993). Used with permission.

3. Eknath Easwaran, introduction to *The Bhagavad Gita* (Petaluma, Calif.: Nilgiri Press, 1985), 4.

Chapter 4

1. Anne Gordon, *A Book of Saints* (New York: Bantam, 1994), 64.

2. Adapted from Eknath Easwaran, comp., *God Makes the Rivers*

to Flow (Tomales, Calif.: Nilgiri Press, 1982), 36. Used with permission.

3. Jon Kabat-Zinn, *Wherever You Go, There You Are* (New York: Hyperion, 1994), 163.

4. Ibid., 49.

5. From his work "In the Vision of God," in *God Makes the Rivers to Flow*, comp. Eknath Easwaran (Tomales, Calif.: Nilgiri Press, 1982), 62.

6. Easwaran, *God Makes the Rivers to Flow*, 12.

7. Starhawk, *The Spiral Dance* (San Francisco: Harper, 1979), 76–77.

8. Herbert Benson, *The Relaxation Response* (New York: Wings, 1975), 145.

9. Deepak Chopra, *Ageless Mind, Timeless Body* (New York: Harmony Books, 1993), 118, 164.

10. Eknath Easwaran, trans., *The Dhammapada* (Tomales, Calif.: Nilgiri Press, 1985), 57.

11. For an excellent detailed account of this method of meditation, see Eknath Easwaran, *Meditation* (Tomales, Calif.: Nilgiri Press, 1991).

Chapter 5

1. Matthew Fox, *Original Blessing* (Sante Fe, N.M.: Bear and Company, 1983), 58.

2. *Philadelphia Inquirer*, 12 February 1995.

3. Susan Faludi, *Backlash* (New York: Crown Publishers, 1991), 203.

4. *University of California at Berkeley Wellness Letter* 10, no. 3 (1993): 1.

5. Abby Adams, comp., *An Uncommon Scold* (New York: Fireside, 1989), 38.

6. *American Health*, 17 March 1987.

7. Eknath Easwaran, comp., *God Makes the Rivers to Flow* (Tomales, Calif.: Nilgiri Press, 1982), 50.

8. Howard J. Clinebell, Jr., *Well Being* (San Francisco: Harper San Francisco, 1992), 76.

9. Norman Ford, *Good Health without Drugs* (New York: St. Martin's Press, 1977), 14–16.

10. *Health Science*, January/February 1995: 8–11.

Chapter 6

1. Eknath Easwaran, trans., *The Dhammapada* (Tomales, Calif.: Nilgiri Press, 1985), 78.

2. *Philadelphia Inquirer*, 9 April 1995.

Chapter 7

1. Rosalie Maggio, comp., *Beacon Book of Quotations by Women* (Boston: Beacon Press, 1992), 13.

2. Lao Tzu, *Tao Te Ching*, trans. Victor Mair (New York: Bantam, 1990).

3. *Time*, 9 October 1995, 64.

4. *Utne Reader*, January/February 1995, 16.

5. Maggio, *Beacon Book of Quotations*, 337. Used with permission.

Chapter 8

1. Carol Newsom and Sharon Ring, eds., *The Women's Bible Commentary* (Louisville: John Knox Press, 1992), 333.

2. J. I. Rodale, *The Synonym Finder*, ed. Laurence Urdang and Nancy LaRoche (Emmaus, Pa.: Rodale Press, 1978), 857.

3. Betty A. DeBerg, *Ungoldly Women: Gender and the First Wave*

of American Fundamentalism (Minneapolis: Augsburg Fortress, 1990), 89.

4. Anne Wilson Schaef, *Women's Reality* (San Francisco: Harper and Row, 1981).

5. Richard Foster, *Study Guide for Celebration of Discipline* (New York: HarperCollins, 1983), 44.

6. Jackie Pflug, *Miles to Go before I Sleep: My Grateful Journey Back from Egypt Air Flight 648* (New York: Hazleden, 1996), 153.

Chapter 9

1. *Story of a Soul: The Autobiography of St. Therese of Lisieux*, trans. John Clarke (Washington, D.C.: Institute of Carmelite Studies, 1972).

2. Anne Bancroft, *The Luminous Vision* (London: Mandala, 1982), 6.

3. Ibid., 7.

4. T. W. Coleman, *English Mystics of the Fourteenth Century* (Westport, Conn.: Greenwood Press, 1991), 141.

5. Frances Beer, *Women and Mystical Experience in the Middle Ages* (Rochester, N.Y.: Boydell and Brewer, 1992), 144–145.

6. Bancroft, *The Luminous Vision*, 66.

7. Carol Flinders, *Enduring Grace* (New York: HarperCollins, 1993), 100

8. Ibid.

9. Shama Futehally, trans., *In the Dark of the Heart* (San Francisco: HarperCollins, 1994). All of Meera's quotes are from this source. Song 13 used with permission.

10. Peace Pilgrim, *Her Life and Work in Her Own Words* (Sante Fe, N.M.: Ocean Tree, 1994), 4.

11. Ibid., 7.

12. Ibid., 21.

13. Ibid., 25.

14. Ann Rush, *Peace Pilgrim: An Extraordinary Life* (Hemet, Calif.: Friends of Peace Pilgrim, 1994), 5.

15. Peace Pilgrim, *Her Life and Work*, 57.

16. Ibid., 91.

Chapter 10

1. Peggy Anderson, comp., *Great Quotes from Great Women* (Lombard, Ill.: Celebrating Excellence, 1992), 3.

2. Maya Angelou, *Wouldn't Take Nothing for My Journey Now* (New York: Bantam, 1993), 17.

3. Norman Vincent Peale, *The Power of Positive Thinking* (New York: Prentice Hall, 1952), 190.

Chapter 11

1. Peggy Anderson, comp., *Great Quotes from Great Women* (Lombard, Ill.: Celebrating Excellence, 1992), 3

2. Philip Novak, *The World's Wisdom* (New York: HarperCollins, 1994), 53.

3. Peace Pilgrim, *Her Life and Work in Her Own Words* (Santa Fe, N.M.: Ocean Tree, 1994), 38.

Bibliography

Adams, Abby, comp. *An Uncommon Scold.* New York: Fireside, 1989.

Anderson, Peggy, comp. *Great Quotes from Great Women.* Lombard, Ill.: Celebrating Excellence, 1992.

Angelou, Maya. *Wouldn't Take Nothing for My Journey Now.* New York: Bantam, 1993.

Bancroft, Anne. *The Luminous Vision.* London: Mandala, 1992.

Beer, Frances. *Women and Mystical Experience in the Middle Ages.* Rochester, N.Y.: Boydell and Brewer, 1992.

Benson, Herbert. *The Relaxation Response.* New York: Wings, 1975.

Brandon, Nathaniel. *The Six Pillars of Self-Esteem.* New York: Bantam, 1994.

Chopra, Deepak. *Ageless Mind, Timeless Body.* New York: Harmony Books, 1993.

Christenson, L. *The Christian Family.* Minneapolis: Bethany House, 1973.

Clinebell, Howard J., Jr. *Well Being.* San Francisco: Harper San Francisco, 1992.

Clinton, Hillary Rodham. *It Takes a Village.* New York: Simon and Schuster, 1996.

Coleman, T. W. *English Mystics of the Fourteenth Century.* Westport, Conn.: Greenwood Press, 1991.

DeBerg, Betty A. *Ungodly Women: Gender and the First Wave of American Fundamentalism.* Minneapolis: Augsburg Fortress, 1990.

Easwaran, Eknath. *The Bhagavad Gita.* Petaluma, Calif.: Nilgiri Press, 1985.

———. *Meditation.* Tomales, Calif.: Nilgiri Press, 1991.

Easwaran, Eknath, comp. *God Makes the Rivers to Flow.* Tomales, Calif.: Nilgiri Press, 1982.

Easwaran, Eknath, trans. *The Dhammapada.* Tomales, Calif.: Nilgiri Press, 1985.

Faludi, Susan. *Backlash.* New York: Crown Publishers, 1991.

Flinders, Carol. *Enduring Grace.* New York: HarperCollins, 1993.

Ford, Norman. *Good Health without Drugs.* New York: St. Martin's Press, 1977.

Foster, Richard. *Study Guide for Celebration of Discipline.* New York: HarperCollins, 1983.

Fox, Matthew. *Original Blessing.* Sante Fe, N.M.: Bear and Company, 1983.

Futehally, Shama, trans. *In the Dark of the Heart.* San Francisco: HarperCollins, 1994.

Gordon, Anne. *A Book of Saints.* New York: Bantam, 1994.

Hauck, Paul. *Overcoming the Rating Game.* Louisville: John Knox Press, 1991.

Jackson, Thomas, ed. *The Works of John Wesley.* Vol. 9. London: John Mason, 1829.

Kabat-Zinn, Jon. *Wherever You Go, There You Are.* New York: Hyperion, 1994.

Lerner, Gerda. *The Creation of Feminist Consciousness.* New York: Oxford University Press, 1993.

Maggio, Rosalie, comp. *Beacon Book of Quotations by Women.* Boston: Beacon Press, 1992.

Nelson, Portia. *There's a Hole in My Sidewalk.* Hillsboro, Oreg.: Beyond Words Publishing, 1993.

Newsom, Carol, and Sharon Ring, eds. *The Women's Bible Commentary.* Louisville: John Knox Press, 1992.

Northrup, Christiane. *Women's Bodies, Women's Wisdom.* New York: Bantam, 1994.

Novak, Philip. *The World's Wisdom.* New York: HarperCollins, 1994.

Peace Pilgrim. *Her Life and Work in Her Own Words.* Santa Fe, N.M.: Ocean Tree, 1994.

Peale, Norman Vincent. *The Power of Positive Thinking.* New York: Prentice Hall, 1952.

Pflug, Jackie. *Miles to Go before I Sleep: My Grateful Journey Back from Egypt Air Flight 648.* New York: Hazleden, 1996.

Rodale, J. I. *The Synonym Finder.* Edited by Laurence Urdang and Nancy LaRoche. Emmaus, Pa.: Rodale Press, 1978.

Rush, Ann. *Peace Pilgrim: An Extraordinary Life.* Hemet, Calif.: Friends of Peace Pilgrim, 1994.

Saint Therese of Lisieux. *Story of a Soul: The Autobiography of St. Therese of Lisieux.* Translated by John Clarke. Washington, D.C.: Institute of Carmelite Studies, 1972.

Sanford, Linda, and Mary Donovan. *Women and Self-Esteem.* New York: Penguin, 1984.

Schaef, Anne Wilson. *Women's Reality.* San Francisco: Harper and Row, 1981.

Smedes, Lewis B. *Forgive and Forget: Healing the Hurts We Don't Deserve.* New York: Pocket Books, 1984.

Smith, Huston. *The World's Great Religions.* New York: Harper-Collins, 1991.

Starhawk. *The Spiral Dance.* San Francisco: Harper, 1979.

Tzu, Lao. *Tao Te Ching.* Translated by Victor Mair. New York: Bantam, 1990.